CW00871112

HOW TO
EMBRACE
PAIN

Published by:
Gita Publishing House
Sadhu Vaswani Mission,
10, Sadhu Vaswani Path,
Pune 411 001, (India).
gph@sadhuvaswani.org

Second Edition

ISBN: 978-93-80743-37-0

Printed by:
Mehta Offset Pvt. Ltd.
Mehta House,
A-16, Naraina Industrial Area II,
New Delhi 110 028, (India).
Phone : +91-11-45670222
info@mehtaoffset.com

HOW TO EMBRACE PAIN

**Prabha Sampath &
Krishna Kumari**

Gita Publishing House
Pune, (India).
www.dadavaswanisbooks.org

Other Books By Dada J.P. Vaswani

In English:

10 Commandments of A Successful Marriage
108 Pearls of Practical Wisdom
108 Simple Prayers of A Simple Man
108 Thoughts on Success
114 Thoughts on Love
A Little Book of Life
A Treasure of Quotes
Around The Camp Fire
Begin The Day With God
Burn Anger Before Anger Burns You
Daily Inspiration
Daily Inspiration (Booklet)
Destination Happiness
Dewdrops of Love
Does God Have Favourites?
Formula For Prosperity
Gateways to Heaven
God In Quest of Man
Good Parenting
I am a Sindhi
In 2012 All Will Be Well
Joy Peace Pills
Kill Fear Before Fear Kills You
Ladder of Abhyasa
Lessons Life Has Taught Me
Life After Death
Management Moment by Moment
Mantras For Peace Of Mind
Many Paths: One Goal
Nearer, My God, To Thee!
New Education Can Make the World New
Peace or Perish
Positive Power of Thanksgiving
Questions Answered
Sadhu Vaswani : His Life And Teachings
Saints For You and Me

Saints With A Difference
Secrets of Health And Happiness
Short Sketches of Saints Known & Unknown
Sketches of Saints Known & Unknown
Stop Complaining: Start Thanking!
Swallow Irritation Before Irritation Swallows You
Teachers are Sculptors
The Little Book of Freedom From Stress
The Little Book of Prayer
The Little Book of Service
The Little Book of Success
The Little Book of Wisdom
The Little Book of Yoga
The Magic of Forgiveness
The Perfect Relationship: Guru and Disciple
The Seven Commandments of the Bhagavad Gita
The Terror Within
The Way of Abhyasa (How To Meditate)
Thus Have I Been Taught
Tips For Teenagers
What You Would Like To know About Hinduism
What You Would Like To know About Karma
Why Do Good People Suffer?
You Are Not Alone God Is With You!

Story Books:

101 Stories For You And Me
25 Stories For Children and also for Teens
Break The Habit
It's All A Matter of Attitude
More Snacks For The Soul
Snacks For The Soul
The Lord Provides
The Heart of a Mother

The King of Kings
The One Thing Needful
The Patience of Purna
The Power of Good Deeds
The Power of Thought
Trust Me All in All or Not at All
Whom Do You Love the Most
You Can Make A Difference

In Hindi:

Aalwar Santon Ki Mahan Gaathaayen
Atmik Jalpaan
Atmik Poshan
Bhakton Ki Uljhanon Kaa Saral Upaai
Bhale Logon Ke Saath Bura Kyon?
Brindavan Ka Balak
Dainik Prerna
Dar Se Mukti Paayen
Ishwar Tujhe Pranam
Jiski Jholi Mein Hain Pyaar
Krodh Ko Jalayen Swayam Ko Nahin
Laghu Kathayein
Mrutyu Hai Dwar... Phir Kya?
Nava Pushp (Bhajans In Hindi and Sindhi)
Prarthna ki Shakti
Pyar Ka Masiha
Sadhu Vaswani: Unkaa Jeevan Aur Shikshaayen
Safal Vivah Ke Dus Rahasya
Santon Ki Leela

In Sindhi:

Burn Anger Before Anger Burns You
Jaade Pireen Kaare Pandh
Munhjee Dil Te Lagee Laahootiyun Saan
Why Do Good People Suffer
Vatan Je Vannan De

Other Books By Dada J.P. Vaswani

In Marathi:
Krodhala Shaanth Kara, Krodhane Ghala Ghalnya Purvee (Burn Anger Before Anger Burns You)
Jiski Jholi Mein Hain Pyaar
Life After Death
Pilgrim of Love
Sind and the Sindhis
Sufi Sant (Sufi Saints of East and West)
What You Would Like To Know About Karma

In Kannada:
101 Stories For You And Me
Burn Anger Before Anger Burns You
Life After Death
Tips for Teenagers
Why do Good People Suffer

In Telugu:
Burn Anger Before Anger Burns You
Life after Death
What You Would Like To Know About Karma

In Arabic:
Daily Appointment With God
Daily Inspiration

In Chinese:
Daily Appointment With God

In Dutch:
Begin The Day With God

In Bahasa:
A Little Book of Success
A Little Book of Wisdom
Burn Anger Before Anger burns You
Life After Death

In Spanish:
Aprenda A Controlar Su Ira (Burn Anger Before Anger burns You)
Bocaditos Para el Alma (Snacks for the Soul)
Dios (Daily Meeting With God)
El Bein Quentu Hagas, Regresa (The Good You Do Returns)
Encontro Diario Com Deus (Daily Appointment With God)
Inicia Tu Dia Con Dios (Begin The Day With God)
L'Inspiration Quotidienne (Daily Inspiration)
Mas Bocaditos Para el Alma (More Snacks for the Soul)
Mata al miedo antes de que el miedo te mate (Kill Fear Before Fear Kills you)
Queme La Ira Antes Que La Ira Lo Queme A Usted(Burn Anger Before Anger Burns You)
Sita Diario ku Dios (I Luv U, God!)
Todo es Cuestion de Actitud! (Its All A Matter of Attitude)
Vida despu'es de la Muerte (Life After Death)

In Gujrati:
Its All A Matter of Attitude

In Oriya:
Burn Anger Before Anger burns You
More Snacks For the Soul
Pilgrim of Love
Snacks For The Soul
Why Do Good People Suffer

In Russian:
What would you like to Know about Karma

In Tamil:
10 Commandments of a Successful Marriage
Burn Anger Before Anger burns You
Daily Appointment with God
Its All a Matter of Attitude
Kill Fear Before Fear Kills You
More Snacks For the Soul
Secrets of Health and Happiness
Snacks For The Soul
Why Do Good People Suffer

In Latvian:
The Magic of Forgiveness

Other Publications:

Recipe Books:
90 Vegetarian Sindhi Recipes
Di-li-cious Vegetarian Recipes
Simply Vegetarian

Books on Dada J. P. Vaswani:
A Pilgrim of Love
Dada J.P. Vaswani: His Life and Teachings
Dada J.P. Vaswani's Historic Visit to Sind
Dost Thou Keep Memory
How To Embrace Pain
Living Legend
Moments with a Master

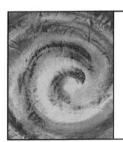

Foreword

Our Beloved Dada's Birthday—
Let's Celebrate it with a Difference!

Happy Birthday, Dearest Dada!

Dada, for you, and for hundreds of thousands of your devotees whose hearts beat every moment by your name, as well as for thousands of friends and admirers who have always regarded you as one of the world's leading spiritual mentors, August 2, 2010, is definitely a birthday with the difference.

In all these years, it was the Mission HQ in Pune which played host to the numerous friends and admirers who came from all over India and all over the world to participate in the week-long celebrations. With due apologies, we must mention that we never, ever heeded to your request that there was no need for elaborate celebrations; each and everyone of us felt that it was *our* birthday, rather than yours! If a stranger had walked into the Mission campus on August 2, he surely would have been bemused to hear hundreds of devotees, volunteers and *satsangis* blithely calling out "Happy Birthday!" to each other, wondering how so many people born on that day, had managed to congregate in one place on their date of birth!

Who can deny that August 2 is indeed a spiritual birthday for all your devotees? Your birth has made all the difference to our lives. We cannot imagine what kind of people we would have been, what kind of lives we would have led without the grace and blessing of your presence. It is entirely fitting therefore, that August 2 is OUR Birthday.

This year, for the first time, we are celebrating our birthday with you in New York, U.S.A. There will of course be week long events, special service programmes and prayers at Pune; we also know, that you will be with the Pune *sangat* too, although in spirit, blessing them with the grace of your love. But your physical presence this year will be with the 'brothers and sisters of America' as Swami Vivekananda once referred to them so memorably.

The reason for this momentous decision is well known to all your friends and admirers worldwide: the fall and major fractures that you sustained on May 7, 2010, during a Sadhana Camp in Panama; and your subsequent hospitalisation for two major orthopaedic surgeries at the Rush Medical Centre in Chicago, U.S.A. And just when things were beginning to look up, we (though in actuality, it was *you*) suffered yet another blow. Soon after the second corrective surgery, which should have been followed immediately by physiotherapy to normalise your limb movements, your body was afflicted with a mild paralytic stroke.

We use the phrase, "your body" advisedly: because it was not you, dear Dada, who were afflicted; it was only your body. As for you, you simply practised the first commandment of the Gita; you just did not identify yourself with the body; in fact, we know you never have! For over two months, we could only watch and pray, as you went through a period of grueling pain, rehabilitative therapy, and 'walked' the arduous road to recovery, each step causing you intense pain.

But through all the pain and suffering, your spirit triumphed; you never once let go of God; you never once let that million dollar smile disappear from your radiant countenance; you never once forgot to thank the Lord for the gift of pain and suffering he had bestowed on you; you never let us forget, even for a moment, that His Will is supreme in our life. The true mentor and master that you are, Dada, you taught us through your personal example, through the excruciating pain and physical suffering that you endured with tremendous fortitude, that **we must never ever run away from pain.**

We may not be happy to admit this, or indeed face up to this fact squarely: but life is fraught with pain for most of us. Escape, running away, giving up, resistance and struggle are of no avail, when pain strikes. But you opened up a new vista, a new option, a valid alternative to escape. **You taught us how to embrace pain with patience, fortitude, acceptance and the spirit of gratitude to God**: we know, Dada, that those magic words, *Thank You God, Thank You God, Thank You God,* were always on your lips and in your heart! We hope that we and others like us, pilgrims on the path of life, will imbibe this valuable lesson in this book which we dedicate to your wonderful spirit of acceptance.

We have heard it said in the Gita, that waters cannot wet, fire cannot burn, swords cannot cleave and wind cannot dry the immortal *atman:* you have shown us that here upon this earth, pain too, does not touch the realised soul. The secret of handling pain is to embrace pain, like a welcome friend! This is the secret we hope to share with all our esteemed readers in this birthday book, which is our offering to you, Dada.

You have always urged us to look at the bright side of things, dear Dada. We have struggled to put this into practice for the last three months or so. A birthday allows no space or time for sadness. So let us assert whole-heartedly, that we are happy and proud that our brothers and sisters in America are being given the blessed opportunity to have you in their midst on your 92nd birthday!

This little book which we offer to you as a special birthday gift, attempts to capture the collective responses and reactions of all your dear ones, the very mixed emotions, the shock, the sadness, the strain, the stress, the pain, the laughter and tears, the highs and lows that we have gone through in reacting to the recent events in the last three months. Today, there is no feeling of regret or disappointment; it is OUR birthday. Today, we will not permit even a shadow of depression or despair to cloud our horizon; it is OUR birthday. Suffice it, that we are celebrating this blessed day, some of us, in your physical presence and proximity, many of us in the firm belief that you are never, ever from us afar – we are never alone, because you are always with us, entwined in our heartbeats, inextricably bound with our thoughts and feelings.

Happy Birthday, Dada!

Prabha Sampath & Krishna Kumari

"It is reported that neurosurgeons are conducting advanced research into methods of alleviating pain with supersonic rays. These are said to be ultra-high frequency sound waves that are used to destroy pain pathways in our brain. I am sure that the practice of silent acceptance, the therapy of cheerfulness and the constant expression of gratitude to God can set in motion spiritual high-frequency waves which will bring God's own healing power to destroy pain. "

J. P. Vaswani

A Constant and Faithful Companion

Dada once narrated to us the real life story of an American lady, about whom he had read in a book. She was described as a delightful, charming person who was always positive. At 94, she continued to remain friendly, cheerful and full of high spirits. They asked her, "What is the secret of your life?"

She replied, "The secret is a very simple one. It is my enthusiasm for life. And because I always think positive, I am positive!"

She paused for a while and then added, "Of course, I owe a lot of my positive thinking to my boyfriends!"

"Boyfriends?" They stared at her in disbelief. "Do you have boyfriends at this age?"

"You bet I do," she replied cheerfully. "They are my constant, faithful companions to this day!"

"Do tell us about them," her friends pleaded.

"I get up each morning with the help of my first boyfriend. He is Will Power. I go out for a walk with my second boyfriend Arth Ritis. Arthritis has been my constant companion for the last 30 years. My evenings are spent with Ben Gay – he has such a soothing presence!"

Here was a lady who was young in spirit! She was a woman of tremendous will power; she suffered from arthritis which can be painful and crippling – but she had learnt to look upon the affliction as a regular companion; and the pain-killing ointment Bengay used widely in the US, had become her healing, soothing friend too!

We cannot help admiring her attitude to life. It is attitude that counts! And so she continued to be young, even at 94! Her secret? She embraced all the pain in her life as a friend!

A DIARY OF EVENTS

May 7
2010

PANAMA

MAY 7

The Sadhana (Spiritual) Camp in Panama commenced on a high note, with great expectations and a mood of jubilation. All the participants eagerly looked forward to this special time with Dada. He greeted each one with a joyous and deep smile, warmly welcoming everyone to a beauteous time to be spent in close proximity with the Divine, away from the fret and fury of worldly life.

The theme that Dada gave for the Camp was: Hujan gad hamesha, na dum bi rahaan dhaar...

He thus entreated to the Beloved Lord:

> May I be ever close to Thee,
> May I perform every act tiny or significant,
> In Thy loving presence.
> May I sleep and wake, eat and work, in awareness of Thee,
> May I share all I have,
> And may I do everything, everything for Thy sake,
> My Beloved!

Thus the entire day of May 7, passed by in a mood of elevation and bliss. At night, around 10 p.m., as Dada was on his way to participate in the campfire that had been organised as part of the day's activities, an unfortunate event came to pass.

As Dada stepped out of the elevator, he saw some children playing ping-pong (table tennis). Dada's child-like heart spontaneously responded to them. So he joined in their game and gleefully played a good volley. Unfortunately, while lobbing one of the shots, Dada stepped backwards, lost his balance, and fell with full force on the hard floor, damaging the right side of his body.

He was in excruciating pain, due to which he could not even be moved from the floor until the ambulance arrived. The devotees gathered around him, and the others hastened to make appropriate arrangements for his care. Dada registered their stressed stances, their faces indicating fear and worry. In return, Dada reflected the same serene smile with which he had initially greeted them, even though the severity of his pain was visible.

The move to the ambulance took its toll. Instead of groaning with pain, Dada would utter 'Hey Ram'. Any one of us would have been wincing with all this pain, our faces completely distorted with agony. Instead, that same steady smile was reflected on Dada's face. The ambulance team was wonder-struck by his attitude. Even during his interaction with the doctors and nurses, the degree of his smile may have varied, either very broad, or *subtly present, but it never left his face, melting the hearts of all those who were with him.*

Across the globe, as text messages and emails flashed on mobile phones and computer screens, we literally felt our hearts breaking. Could this be really happening to us – to our beloved Dada? What could we do? How were we supposed to face this calamity? How could God inflict such great pain on our beloved Master? Why, he had just about recovered from his shoulder injury which he sustained in January! This could not be, it really could not be! O how we wished all this was but a bad dream and not really true!

Contents

CHAPTER

1

We Love You, Dada!

His magic is his unconditional love. His mission in life is selfless service. His vision for the future is – a world without war; a world without want; a world without violence. His dream: Peace, Unity and Brotherhood among people and nations. His sacred *mantra*: "Reverence for all life". His one teaching for all of us: "Turn back to God". His one advice to one and all: "Cast all your burdens upon the Lord. Joyfully accept His Will: Live a carefree life". He is a mentor, guide and guardian to thousands of aspiring hearts and souls. He remarks in utter humility: "I am a disciple of all seekers; master to none!" His life is his message.

Why do we love Dada so unconditionally, so profoundly, above and beyond all our worldly relationships and material concerns?

The answer is very simple: Dada is all things to all people; he is never 'distant' or 'remote' from our genuine fears, worries, insecurities and problems. He understands our needs; he empathises with our conditions; he is always willing to show us the way forward…

The spiritual needs and aspirations of the modern age are perhaps far more complex than the genuine quest of past generations, who were fortunate to lead lives that were less complicated. We are trapped in a rat race which is not of our own making; we are victims of the vagaries of inflation and the stock market; our lives are changed by distant wars and recurring incidents of terrorism taking place all around the globe; our parents feel let down and betrayed by us; our children seem to speak a different language from us; our friends and families seem to make more demands on us than we can cope with; it is frightening to make sense of our lives at times.

What is happening to us? Where are we heading? Are we fulfilling the purpose of this life, or simply drifting from moment to moment, event to event, crisis to crisis? Some of us actually begin to avoid being left alone with our thoughts…

To our confused generation, with its multitude of complex problems, wants, needs, ambitions and aspirations, Dada offers hope – tempered with love, understanding, compassion and wisdom. So what if we cannot cope? So what if our brains refuse to function effectively? So what if we are overwhelmed by emotions and feelings which we are unable to control? He offers us an understanding heart and wise counsel; he teaches us to have faith in God and in the universe around us; he tells us about the magic of prayer; he assures us that each one of us is unique and special, and that we have a special purpose to fulfill in this life; it is this combination of love and wisdom, spirituality and faith, compassion and pure understanding, this unique integrity of head and heart and spirit that makes Dada's presence so reassuring in our lives.

Dada is all things to all people: high-powered businessmen and entrepreneurs take his opinion and advice before they make major moves; senior citizens consult him about their spiritual aspirations; young executives seek his wise counsel to help plan their careers; mothers, fathers, spouses, siblings and sons and daughters seek his help to mend troubled relationships; seekers after true knowledge know they can rely on him for guidance; you can even see the little ones waiting to meet him with their pencils, so that their efforts in the examination may be blessed with his grace!

Dada is genuinely caring and loving; he does not dismiss people's fears and insecurities as foolish or worthless; nor is he content to offer 'sops' to all our unreasonable demands; if we approach him with unreasonable, unfair, malicious or selfish demands, he is the firm and fair mentor who will urge us to quit wrong doing and wrong thinking, and gently and firmly lead us back on the right track. No one who has gone to him with petty cavils and selfish complaints ever got any satisfaction out of their gripes

We cannot find our Guru. It is he who will come and find us. And when he does, you will feel blessed and ecstatic. "This is my Guru!" you will exclaim in rapture. "He is the one that I have been waiting for all these years! My Blessed Master, why were you away from me for so long?" He, in his grace, will find you.

-J.P. Vaswani

and grouses: the steel grip of his wisdom under the velvet glove of his compassion will surely and quickly bring us back to good sense!

What is it that Dada offers to people?

We have the benefit of his wisdom, which is both inborn, intuitive, instinctive as well as enhanced and empowered by a brilliant scholarship and wide and deep reading. We have the comfort of knowing that he is not only wise, but loving and sympathetic; his compassion and understanding endear him to us even more; and the light of God's grace and the Guru's blessing shines in those radiant eyes! Above all, he offers us hope and faith and optimism; he assures us that we are never alone; he is a constant, living, moving reminder of God's presence in this world; he assures us that we can talk to God directly, as and when we want; he assures us too, that God is always listening to us, always watching us, always watching over us. You are all princes and princesses, he reminds us: you are the children of the King of kings! Life is God's gift to you; each new day is His vote of confidence in you; and true happiness is your birthright! Claim it as your inheritance from your heavenly Father!

He who loves the Guru fears to do anything that may displease his master. Whatever he does, he does out of the pure unsullied devotion arising in his heart for the Guru.

-J.P. Vaswani

Nor do we all have to have a private audience with Dada to get answers to our pressing questions. Dada knows us; he anticipates our needs and problems and has solutions even before we can define our difficulties. Watch the congregation at his *ruh rihans* and special *satsangs*: you will see the devotees in rapt attention, very often with tears flowing from their eyes, or the joy of realisation and awareness lighting up their countenances. Most of them will tell you that they came to the *satsang* with a pressing problem, a difficult emotional crisis or in despair and distress, only hoping that a glimpse of their beloved Dada would somehow, miraculously alleviate their misery: not only has their hope been justified, but in most cases, in the course of his talk, Dada has touched upon their crisis, indicated a way out, pointed in the direction of a solution to their problems! He has uttered words that seemed specifically addressed to them, and they feel suddenly light and relieved at having discovered their remedy from his spoken words!

He understands us; he loves us; he knows what is good for us; and he unfailingly indicates this to us! We don't even have to knock: the door is opened for us. We don't even have to ask aloud: it is given to us freely and unstintingly!

Ishwar, mata, pita, bandhu, sakha and above all, the kind and compassionate Guru – is he not all things to all of us? Is it any wonder that we should love him so deeply, so excessively, so much more than anything else or anyone else?

Memorable Moments With Dada

Everyday, in his hospital room, Dada would hold a little *satsang* for the brothers and sisters who were with him. Sometimes, a passing doctor or nurse would stop by to join the gathering. They said they found the vibrations in the satsang positive and healing.

One day, Dada gave the thought: Don't make me *Manmukh,* make me *Gurmukh.*

There are two kinds of people, he explained to the brothers and sisters; the first kind are called *gurmukh,* and the second are called *manmukh.* *Gurmukh* are those whose face is always turned to the Guru, even as the sunflower from the earth, follows the direction of the sun as it traverses the sky. Such people are always living and moving and speaking and thinking and acting in the consciousness of the Guru's presence with them, within them. They will never ever do anything, of which they think the Guru would disapprove. The Guru might be thousands of miles away; but their minds and hearts are focused on him all the time, under all circumstances. Before every decision, before every deed,

> The Guru might be thousands of miles away; but their minds and hearts are focused on him all the time, under all circumstances.

they ask themselves: what would the Guru have me do in this situation? And they act accordingly.

The *manmukh* are those people who tend to be led away by their worldly desires; they often fall prey to their own greed, covetousness, lust, hatred, and the like. The *manmukh* person thinks he is happy, but he is not really happy. He may have all the wealth of the world, but true happiness will elude him. The *gurmukh* person may be poor in the wealth of the world, but he will always be happy.

Dada then narrated the story of Sananda, the devoted disciple of Adi Shankara. Sananda was envied by the other disciples, who felt that he was being singled out as the dearest disciple of the Guru. They thought that he did not deserve this honour. Sri Shankara heard them expressing their envy and resentment, and decided to show them Sananda's true worth.

One day, as the Master and his disciples were walking along the banks of the river Ganga, Sri Shankara called out to Sananda, who was standing on the opposite bank, "Come here to me, immediately, as fast as you can." Without even a moment's hesitation, Sananda closed his eyes, and started walking across the swirling waters of the Ganga. It was the rainy season, and the river was in spate; the other disciples watched in disbelief, as Sananda rushed across the flowing waters, to reach the Guru as quickly as he could.

Without even a moment's hesitation, Sananda closed his eyes, and started walking across the swirling waters of the Ganga.

A miracle came to pass before their wide-open eyes. Ganga Mata made a full blown lotus appear beneath Sananda's feet, each time he took a step forward. Thus stepping across a veritable bridge of lotuses, Sananda arrived by the Guru's side, breathless but ready to be of service.

Thus it was that Sananda came to be known as Padmapada or the 'One at whose feet the lotus blooms'.

Padmapada was a *gurmukh*. The Guru's word, the Guru's command was to him the ultimate duty. Therefore, he was the most beloved disciple of his Guru.

> The Guru's word, the Guru's command was to him the ultimate duty. Therefore, he was the most beloved disciple of his Guru.

There were two friends. They grew up alongside one another; they studied in the same school together. They would eat together, play together, go out together. But after graduation, their ways parted, and each went his own way. One of them took up his family business and became very wealthy. In fact, he became the richest man in the town. The other one remained poor, but he joined the *satsang*, became an ardent devotee of the Guru, and was happy and thrilled to be a member of the Guru's *satsang*. He was an enthusiastic participant in all the activities and service programmes of the congregation.

Years passed; and towards the close of their life, in the autumn of their days, the two friends met. They embraced one another fondly, filling in the gaps that time had brought about in their friendship. Each one told the other what

How to Embrace Pain

they had been doing with their lives, and how life had treated them. The *gurmukh* warmly congratulated his friend on the success he had made of his family business. But the wealthy man protested. "What I have achieved is nothing," he said. "As the years go by, I realise that true wealth is not what I have earned. True wealth is what you have earned. When we complete our journey here and go to God, do remember me in heaven. For I am sure that you will be the privileged one there! I was busy chasing wealth, while you were seeking the treasures of the spirit under your Guru's protective shelter. You have done the right thing, for you have made a success of this human life. As for me, it is perhaps too late now to do what you have done...Therefore, I beg you, remember me in heaven..."

"*Remember me in heaven*," Dada added, "are the very words that the thief crucified on the cross spoke to Jesus, before he died. *Remember me in heaven*; and Jesus said to him, "Your sins are forgiven, you shall be with me in paradise."

The little congregation in the hospital room was quiet in the spirit of reflection. Most of us run after worldly things. Very few there are who realise the value of spiritual wealth, and try to gather it.

"Don't make me *manmukh*, make me *gurmukh*," Dada concluded. "This should be the prayer that every parent should teach his child. Don't make me *manmukh*, make me *gurmukh*."

"Don't make me *manmukh*, make me *gurmukh*," Dada concluded. "This should be the prayer that every parent should teach his child. Don't make me *manmukh*, make me *gurmukh*."

A DIARY OF EVENTS

May 8-11
2010

CHICAGO

Dada was airlifted in an air-ambulance, which was equipped with all the necessary instruments, and also had on board a doctor and a nurse, to take care of him. Despite his own pain and acute discomfort, Dada kept enquiring about the comfort of the medical staff, expressing his concern for them. The plane landed safely at Chicago.

Doctors in Chicago revealed that Dada had fractured the right hip (femur bone), the right shoulder (humerus bone) and the right elbow (olecranon). As treating all this would require major surgery, Dada's delicate condition was first stabilised. The slightest movement caused intense pain, but Dada continued to be cheerful, ever smiling and relaxed.

MAY 10 °

The first surgery took place on Dada's hip and shoulder. It was performed by **Dr. Walter Virkus.** As so many areas had been injured on the same side, the surgery had to be performed with extreme care and sensitivity. A rod and two screws (intramedullary nails) were inserted into the femur bone. A plate and multiple screws were inserted in the humerus bone. As we may well imagine, the levels of pain must have been very high; but Dada, with his patience and perseverance, retained his trade-mark smile.

By God's grace the operation went off successfully. When he was wheeled out, Dada could see the strained and tense faces of all his devotees. With a gentle smile he constantly recited the words, "Gratitude to Thee, O Lord. Let me bear this for Thy sake. I accept this gift from You gladly. Tere Liye, Tere Liye."

Even under these extreme conditions, our beloved Guru continues to be a living example for all that we should aspire to be!

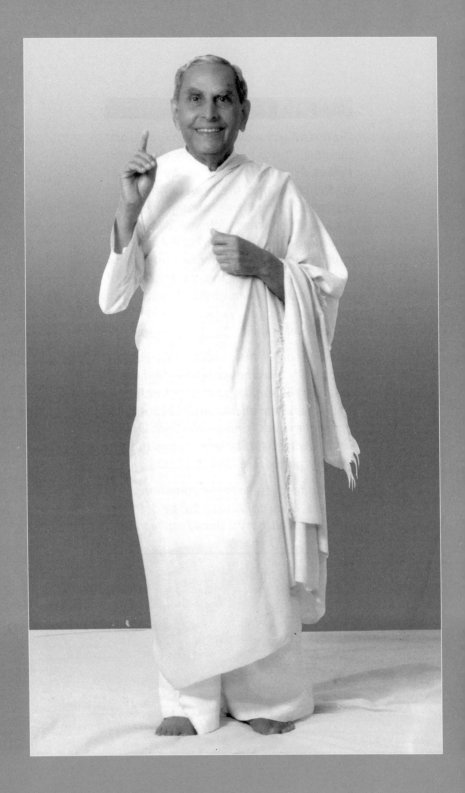

CHAPTER

2

What Dada Teaches Us?

We live by his words; we take each breath by his grace; he is our friend, philosopher and guide; he is the sustaining support of our life; he makes our life worth living; he gives us hope of liberation and freedom from the cycle of life and death.

How can we ever hope to tell you in a few printed pages all that he teaches us? And that too, at a time when our 'learning' is being put to the stiffest test by what he is going through?

There is only one way in which we can even attempt to do this. We can share with you Dada's wisdom in his own words.

"The one lesson we all need to learn," Dada tells us again and again, "is utter dependence on God."

His constant reminder to us is: "You are not alone; God is with you."

His formula for happiness: "Let your desires tend towards God and terminate in Him!"

His repeated *mantra* for all of us: "Accept! Accept! Accept the Will of the Lord."

The purpose of life, according to Dada: To live and glorify God; to serve His suffering children (not forgetting that birds and animals, too, are His children!)

The four simple rules of life, as taught by Dada are: 1. Be simple in dress, diet and daily living. 2. Be pure as the lotus in the lake. 3. Be prayerful as the daisy that ever turns to the sun. 4. Be helpful to as many as you can.

The teachings of all the great ones is consistent with Truth. If at all there are any contradictions, they exist only in our minds. Therefore, we must try and understand the teachings of the great ones, not merely with our minds, but with the higher intellect and the heart.

-J.P. Vaswani

Dada's favourite prayer, which we hold close to our hearts: "God, make me pure, make me useful, make me harmless! Make me an instrument of Thy help and healing in this world of suffering and pain!"

Dada's formula for plenty and prosperity: Rely on the Lord alone! Turn to Him for all your needs and you will lack nothing!

The secret of happiness, according to Dada: "If you want to be happy, make others happy!" The happiness that goes out of you will return to you a hundred fold. Such is the Law. Therefore, do at least one good deed of service every day.

Dada's positive secret of health: choose as your personal physicians, Dr. Diet, Dr. Quiet, Dr. Laughter and Dr. Sunshine!

Dada's nutrition tip: "*Kam khao, gam khao.*" Eat little: Do not react, always respond to any situation.

The best therapy for a harmonious life, according to Dada: the therapy of thanksgiving.

The secret of perfection, according to Dada: Make all that you do, an offering unto the Lord!

The Lord's injunction to us is quite clear: "Go to the great ones," he tells us. "Surrender to them; devote yourself to them; ask of them; and they will impart the knowledge to you."

-J.P. Vaswani

The most important among the senses, according to Dada: the sixth sense i.e. the sense of humour.

The perfect relationship, according to Dada: the *Guru-shishya* relationship.

Here are some invaluable pearls of Dada's wisdom:

"May I touch everything with love, treat everyone with respect."

"Let go, let go, let God!"

"If only everyone in the world would spend just five minutes in silence everyday, our world would become new!"

"No price is too high to save a single life."

"Man's greatest tragedy is – he thinks he has plenty of time."

"My religion is the religion of unity and love, service and sacrifice."

"The woman represents Goddess Lakshmi. Therefore, treat her with respect."

"Whatever you give in the pure love of God, in the service of the poor and broken ones, that is deposited in your account in the Bank of Heaven. It is the Bank that never fails, the Bank that outlives death. What you credit here will be your true and lasting treasure, your wealth for eternity."

"It is not religion which has failed man: it is man who has failed religion."

"You may have a hundred other appointments to keep everyday: but whatever you do, do not fail to keep your daily appointment with God."

"Change your attitude and you can change the pattern of your life."

"There are a hundred-and-one ways of doing a thing, but only one way is the best. See that you do everything in the best way possible."

"The day on which I have not learnt something new, is a lost day indeed."

"Let us not plan anything; let us allow the Will of God to guide us."

"Time is the most precious of all our possessions. Therefore, let us not remain idle, even for a single moment. Take care of every moment, every minute."

"Work not for wages! When you work for money, work becomes boredom. Therefore, work for the pure love of God and for the love of suffering humanity."

"Peace does not depend on outer things, but resides within the soul: therefore, man must find peace within himself."

"The test of a man is: how much he can bear and how much he can share and how soon he confesses a mistake and makes amends for it."

"The right to live is not only a fundamental human right; it is also the first fundamental right of every animal. No man can take away that which he cannot give. Since we cannot give life to a dead creature, we cannot take away the life of a living one!"

"Wars will not cease until all killing is stopped. No sentient creature must be killed. For if a man kills an animal for food, he will not hesitate to kill a fellow-human whom he regards as an enemy. Therefore, we must grow in the spirit of reverence for all life. All life must be regarded as sacred."

"The time has come when we must decide that all forms of exploitation must cease. We must recognise the moral inviolability of the individual – both human and non-human. Animals do not exist as resources for human beings. All types of human tyranny, all forms of cruelty and slaughter must cease if we are to have lasting peace upon this earth."

"God is One, but the ways to reach Him are many."

"The one way to know God is to love Him."

"There is no Hindu and no Mussalman, no Christian and no Jew. We all are children of the One Heavenly Father, the One Divine Mother of the Universe."

"As I have studied the different religions of the world and the teachings of their great founders, I have found a beautiful similarity in their message. To study different religions in the spirit of sympathy and understanding is to know that each one of them emphasises the same fundamental truth. No religion is superior to another."

"Make God a reality in your life. Awaken love for the Divine in your hearts. A human being without love is like a hive without honey, a flower without fragrance. Therefore, love God with your mind, heart and soul."

"Man does not live by the beats of his heart, but by the grace of God. Let our lives be rooted in the Holy Name of God, and we will discover that the human body is but a garment we have worn. You are not the body; you are the immortal *atman* within. *Tat twam asi!* That art Thou!"

Memorable Moments With Dada

Allah dado athyee: mattan ko seeno sahai..

"The Lord is Almighty," Dada said, translating the thought for the day. "The Lord is strong, so let no one think of battling with the Will of God."

Dada added, after a pause: "Let us remember too, that the Lord is precious, He is so gentle, He is also good, kind, and infinitely compassionate."

> If we realise that God is the Prime Mover, and the Source of all action, it becomes easy for us to surrender to His Divine Will, and thus become free from the clutches of the ego.

In ancient India, a school of ascetics believed in pre-ordained fate, and taught their followers to take life as events presented themselves, for individual effort was useless under the circumstances. Newer faiths like Buddhism and Jainism dismissed the whole concept of fate and placed the utmost emphasis on individual effort. It is only Hinduism, Dada explained, that combines the ideals of free will and Divine Will, to show that although man is the architect of his own destiny, he must always submit to the Divine Will. If we realise that God is the Prime Mover, and the Source of all action, it becomes easy for us to surrender to His Divine Will, and thus become free from the clutches of the ego.

The *Gayatri mantra* which is recited with piety and devotion by millions of Hindus, is at once an adoration, a meditation and prayer, acknowledging the power of the Divine Will. Here is a free translation of this powerful *mantra*:

> O God, the Protector, the basis of all life, Who is self-existent, Who is free from all pains and Whose contact frees the soul from all troubles, Who pervades the Universe and sustains all, the Creator and Energiser of the whole Universe, the Giver of happiness, Who is worthy of acceptance, the most excellent, Who is Pure and the Purifier of all, let us embrace that very God, so that He may direct our mental faculties in the right direction.

Our ancient epics and *Puranas* too illustrate the power of Divine Will: thus the Pandavas represent human free will operating in consonance with Divine Will; while the Kauravas represent human free will set against Divine Will. So it is that the Kurukshetra war is described as a battle between good and evil, *dharma* and *adharma*. When Arjuna wavers momentarily before the battle, the Lord gives His Divine teachings to him; significantly, towards the end of his discourse, Sri Krishna actually tells Arjuna: *"yadechasi tada kuru"* – "(I have told you all that I had to say) Do as you desire to do." Arjuna might choose to act as he wished; but the death and destruction of the Kauravas was pre-destined: it was the death of *adharma,* according to the Divine Will.

So it is that the Kurukshetra war is described as a battle between good and evil, *dharma* and *adharma.*

Arjuna was merely the instrument; Sri Krishna was the Doer. So too with most

How to Embrace Pain

of our actions: events and incidents are pre-determined according to the Divine Will; our reaction, our response, our attitude to these events and incidents is of our free will. Our *Karma* is determined not so much by our actions, as by the attitude with which we perform actions.

A DIARY OF EVENTS

May 11 - 17
2010

CHICAGO

MAY 11

On the day following the surgery, May 11, Dada was responding well to the post-operative care and treatment. The hospital that Dada is being treated at is known as the Rush Medical Centre at Chicago, which is one of the best hospitals, with state of art equipment. The doctors are well experienced, and the entire paramedical staff is well-trained. They are all kind, polite, patient, outgoing and friendly. This medical facility is a tertiary centre in orthopaedic treatment. All arrangements for Rev. Dada's treatment have been made with the kind assistance of **Dr. Ramesh Chhablani.** *Dada refers to him as an angel of God who has been sent to this earth for us, for he has the sensitivity of feeling the pain of another. This dedicated doctor renders caring treatment not only to Dada, whom he reveres as a Guru and father, but towards all his other patients too. Each and* everyone of his colleagues, and other doctors, nurses and patients speak highly of him.

Dada, having undergone two painful and traumatic procedures, yet had a countenance which radiated his inner peace and a demeanour of joyful acceptance. The doctors, nurses and the occupational therapist who have come in contact with Dada marvel at his forbearance even in the face of so much physical suffering. Dada is thankful that the procedures have gone through smoothly. He believes that Divine Grace has turned a mountain into a molehill.

Physiotherapy for Dada began immediately the day after surgery. The doctors advocate that physiotherapy is the most important component for healing. Without the instant follow-up of physiotherapy, all the efforts of surgery are in vain. The latter is only corrective, but it is the former which accomplishes mobility and normalcy.

As characteristic of him, Dada's sense of humour surfaces even during these difficult times, for he never believes in being gloomy and low. When nurse Jill said that she was sorry about Dada's fall, he replied, "It is a rise, not a fall. Just as a child rises up after a fall, so too, I have risen."

When the orthopaedic surgeon, **Dr. Walter Virkus**, was explaining to Dada the details of the procedure he was going to perform on him, Dada merely said, "The doctor can perform procedures and prescribe but it is God who heals!"

CHAPTER

3

When We Are Put To The Test

At the mere mention of the words, "You have to take a test", nine out of ten people are likely to get stressed. We are not just talking about students, but even executives, civil servants, bank officers and senior lecturers, who may be required to take eligibility/promotion/increment related tests in the course of their careers and feel the same way.

Guru-bhakti involves unconditional surrender, absolute faith and devoted service to the Guru; this naturally includes utter obedience to the Guru's wishes, bearing witness to his teachings in deeds of daily living.

-J.P. Vaswani

A test is demanding – physically, intellectually and psychologically. We are anxious to do well, 'show off' our best in terms of performance, and this of course adds to the stress!

Some of us have our own tried and tested 'techniques' to 'clear' a test. We plan to work on selected topics and omit others. We attempt 'four out of six' questions, hoping to focus on our own strong areas, instead of wasting time answering all questions.

Life does not permit such 'options'. We cannot leave out this section or another when life puts us to the test; we cannot exercise selective choice. We have to attempt all the questions and 'pass' the test. Devoted disciples do not like to fail the test of their Guru's teachings! What is more, the true disciple cannot be content with 50% or 60% marks in the test of spirituality and personal evolution for only 100% is good enough for the Guru!

The Guru, let us remember, is omniscient; he knows us even better than we know ourselves. Then why does he allow our spiritual mettle to be tested? Why does he need to see if we have imbibed his teachings well?

The answer is simple to ignite and make us discover our true potential and to show us exactly where we stand; and, perhaps, to show the others what our true potential is.

If there is one thing we are all justifiably proud and happy of, it is our identity as devotees/disciples of Rev. Dada. In his infinite kindness and magnanimity, Dada has accepted us into his fold, allowed us to call ourselves his "fellow disciples", although he constantly reiterates: "I am the Guru of none; I am a disciple of all. I am but a pilgrim on the path, in the company of fellow pilgrims." In his intimate spiritual discourses, he actually addresses us as his dear brothers and sisters.

But has it ever occurred to us to ask ourselves: am I worthy to lisp the name of my Master? Am I fit to be called his devotee or disciple? Is my conduct, my behaviour, my attitude to life, my treatment of those with whom I come into contact befitting of one who stands before the world as Rev. Dada J. P. Vaswani's disciple?

The Guru, as we said, is omniscient: I cannot retract from his teachings because he is not in my vicinity; I cannot break his golden rules of conduct because he cannot see me or hear me; I cannot do as I please because I am abroad or because he is in another corner of the world!

Obviously, this stipulation is not for 'casual' visitors to the *satsang,* or people who 'mark attendance' at Rev. Dada's programmes. We are talking about people who love him, revere him and look up to him as their guide and guardian and mentor, their spiritual teacher. For those of us who claim this privilege, the 'test' is different; it is 'tougher' than the rest.

To put it briefly, every thought we think, every word we utter, every action we perform, each and every reaction we offer to external circumstances must bear witness to the Guru's teachings. We are not sages or saints, like the Masters; nor are we evolved beings who have seen the light; but we are, and we must ever remain true seekers – seekers after spiritual growth, seekers after perfection, seekers after eventual liberation.

———

In ancient times men who aspired to liberation had to undertake several austerities and penances so that they might conquer the senses and passions and attain the spiritual fitness that is a pre-requisite for self-realization. Alas, how many of us in this day and age can undertake such gaur tapasya?

-J. P. Vaswani

———

Seekers like us cannot get away with pass marks in the test of life! Perfection, or at least excellence should be our goal.

"Excuse me," some of you may feel like interjecting at this point, "but why should we be put to a test? Isn't that harsh and strict and unkind?

On the other hand, it is actually God's kindness and the Guru's great concern for us that puts us to these tests – it is so that we understand ourselves, grow in self-realisation and develop spiritual strength. In other words, it is for our own spiritual well being. Taking these spiritual tests will help us grow in wisdom, understanding and faith.

All along, we have been blissfully content to drink the nectar of Dada's wisdom, to taste the ambrosial sweetness of his profound understanding of the truth of life. This experience is undoubtedly delightful; but the experience of putting those teachings into practice, bearing witness to them in acts of daily life will bring us far greater joy and fulfillment! By doing this we pass on to the next higher level, and that is truly an elevating experience!

At a time when our faith and conviction are severely tested, it is good to remind ourselves the pain and suffering that our beloved Guru has taken on in the recent past. In his kindness, he has taken on the pain and suffering, and demonstrated too, the positive response and attitude to it.

What can we do as his disciples?

Practise the power of prayer that he has always emphasised; utter the Name of God to invoke the Divine healing power, for he has always taught us that the Name of the Lord is as great if not greater than the Lord Himself; read/recite those holy scriptures and *mantras*, about the magic vibrations of which he has told us again and again; go into silence, to communicate with God, for Dada calls silence the language of devotion and prayer; and above all, offer little and big acts of service to the poor and the needy, for in them our Master beholds the reflection of the Divine Face.

And yet, and yet, what a magnanimous Guru he is! It is said that God puts his devotees through terrible personal trials and tribulations to strengthen their faith; is it not Dada's magnanimity that he has allowed himself to pass through such pain and tribulation that we may pass the test of faith?

Now, can we allow ourselves to fail this test?

Memorable Moments With Dada

Q: "Dada, in yesterday's *upadesh*, you told us to talk sweetly and gently to everyone we interact with. Before I promise myself to do that, Dada, I would like to ask you a question. We meet so many people everyday; people who work with us, colleagues and subordinates in the office... sometimes, we are expected to deal strictly with them, in the interests of the organisation. What are we to do, Dada? Talk to them sweetly and gently, or firmly and strictly?"

Dada: "There must be no compromise with your *dharma*, your duty. So I say to you, if it is your duty to speak strictly or even a little harshly with someone, you must do it. Speak sweetly to everyone, except if it is your duty to do otherwise.

The Gita opens with the word duty. *Dharma kshetrey Kurukshetrey*, those are the opening words of the Bhagavad Gita. *Dharma Kshetrey, Dharma* means duty, *Kshetrey* means field. This life is our *Kurukshetra,* our Field of duty. Like Arjuna, we are called upon to do our duty, practise our *swadharma* here. This is the ultimate test of one who is true to the Lord's Will: he must do his duty,

This life is our *Kurukshetra,* our Field of duty. Like Arjuna, we are called upon to do our duty, practise our *swadharma* here.

How to Embrace Pain

unfailingly, uncomplainingly, without any expectation of reward, without fear or favour.

But, let me add, talk gently, walk humbly on the pathways of life. This is expected of us all."

Dada then narrated the story of *Yaksha prashna,* found in the *Aranya Parva* of the epic, the Mahabharata. When the Pandavas were living in exile, in the forest, they were approached by a poor Brahmin, whose *arani* sticks (i.e. fire-drilling sticks) had been taken away by a fleeing crane; without the sticks, he could not perform his daily havan; in desperation, he appealed to the Pandava princes to restore his *arani* sticks to him.

Yudhishtra realised that as kshatriyas, it was their duty to come to the aid of deserving brahmins; so the five brothers set off into the forest, in hot pursuit of the crane. They spotted the bird soon enough; but it dodged them, led them hither and thither, and finally disappeared into a thickly wooded area. By now, the princes were exhausted, irritated and very thirsty indeed.

Yudhishtra bade his younger brother, Nakula, to climb a nearby tree and scout for some sign of a water source. Nakula climbed the tree, and saw a clear pool of water, some distance away. He offered to his brothers that he would go and fetch water for all of them, and urged them to rest for a while in the shade of the tree. His elder brothers gladly agreed.

Talk gently, walk humbly on the pathways of life. This is expected of us all.

Very soon, Nakula reached the pool. He was about to scoop up a handful of water and drink it, when he heard a disembodied voice say to him: "Before you touch this water, my dear child, you must first answer my questions."

Nakula was taken aback; he looked all around the pool, but could see no one. He decided to ignore the warning, and touched the water; instantly, he fell dead.

In a short while, Sahadeva followed his brother: the same experience befell him; he too, ignored the warning and touched the water; he too, fell dead.

Finding that Nakula and Sahadeva did not return, Arjuna took up his bow and arrow, and went to the pool. Shocked to see his brothers dead, he was about to step into the pool, when the same polite voice interrupted him: "Before you touch this water, my dear child, you must first answer my questions."

He decided to ignore the warning, and touched the water; instantly, he fell dead.

Blind with rage, he shouted back: "Whoever you are, you cowardly, murderous spirit, I dare you to show yourself to me. Stop me if you can." Ignoring the repeated warnings of the voice, he shot several arrows in the direction of the voice, and tried to drink the water. He too, embraced the same deadly fate as his brothers.

Bhima followed him, and the angry encounter was repeated. Bhima too, lost his temper, and tried to attack the spirit; he also fell dead, on touching the waters of the pool.

How to Embrace Pain

Worried and concerned for his brothers, Yudhishtra arrived on the scene, and was dismayed to find his four brothers lying dead by the pool. His heart was broken, and he began to lament the loss of his dear ones. There were no wounds on any of the bodies; no marks of violence. It must be a supernatural being who had killed them, he surmised. Wiping away his tears, he went to the pool to get some water, to begin the last rites of his brothers. Then he too, heard a voice: "I am he who killed your brothers. You shall be my fifth victim, if you do not answer my questions."

"Noble one, you are no ordinary spirit," Yudhishtra replied, "for I know that no *gandharva* or *rakshasa* could have taken on my brave brothers and killed them thus. I beg you, reveal your identity to me, and tell me why you have killed my brothers and what you want of me."

The voice replied, "May you be blessed, Yudhishtra. I am a *yaksha,* and you may see me now." A form began to reveal itself before his eyes, and the prince saw that it was a massive figure with eyes like fire, and a voice like thunder. "I am the Lord of this pool, and I warned your brothers that they should not enter these waters without my permission. They defied me, and thus met their fate. If you want to touch these waters, be warned that you too, must answer my questions first."

"O noble spirit, I have no desire to touch what is not mine," replied Yudhishtra, with great courtesy and humility. "Ask your questions, and I shall try and answer them to the best of my ability."

Then he too, heard a voice: "I am he who killed your brothers. You shall be my fifth victim, if you do not answer my questions."

Thus began the yaksha *prashna* – an interlocution between Dharmaputra, as he was called, and the *yaksha*. This question-answer session is regarded by scholars as an episode that distils the very essence of Hindu *dharma*. The *yaksha* flung question after tough question at the Pandava prince; and with hands folded in devotion, bowing humbly to the spirit, Dharmaputra answered one question after another, carefully, thoughtfully and courteously.

At the end of the grueling question-answer session, the *yaksha* said to Yudhishtra, "I am well pleased by your wisdom, and even more pleased by your kind and gentle nature. You may ask me for a boon, and I shall grant it to you."

Yudhishtra bowed his head in gratitude, and said to the *yaksha*, "I pray you, bring my brother Nakula back to life."

The *yaksha* was amazed. "I granted you just one boon; why did you choose to ask for the life of your step brother, when you could have chosen the valiant Arjuna or the mighty Bhima, who are your own brothers?"

"We, the Pandavas, are the sons of Pandu from his two queens, Kunti and Madri. I have been spared by you, and it is only fair that a son of Madri should also live to share the future with me. Therefore, I asked for Nakula to be brought to life. That is true *dharma*, and *dharma*, is dearer to me than all else."

The *yaksha* was mightily pleased with Yudhishtra. "I will never see the like of

> I am well pleased by your wisdom, and even more pleased by your kind and gentle nature. You may ask me for a boon, and I shall grant it to you.

How to Embrace Pain

you ever again," he said. "In your wisdom, intelligence, humility, sense of duty, and righteousness, you are unsurpassed. I am glad to reveal my identity to you. I am none other than your father, the Lord of *Dharma*. I grant you the lives of all four of your brothers. May you prosper in all that you undertake."

"May I ask one more boon of you?" asked Yudhishtra in all humility. "Please grant that I may overcome six of my most deadly enemies: lust, anger, avarice, possessiveness, arrogance and envy. Please grant that I may ever be led in search of truth."

"My dear child, you ask for that which you already have. Go in peace and be assured that your troubles are all over."

Yudhishtra was surely one who walked humbly and spoke gently!

Please grant that I may overcome six of my most deadly enemies: lust, anger, avarice, possessiveness, arrogance and envy. Please grant that I may ever be led in search of truth.

A DIARY OF EVENTS

May 17-18
2010

CHICAGO

By God's grace, on May 17, Dada's second surgery on his right elbow went well without a hitch. It was performed by **Dr. Mark Cohen.** *It was a long and complicated procedure, which lasted for over three hours. The hearts of the devotees accompanying Dada beat heavier and faster, but they were shored up with prayers and with trust in the expertise of the surgeons. The doctors emerged from the operation theatre totally satisfied with the way the surgery had proceeded.*

Prior to the surgery, the doctors had asked Dada if he was comfortable. Dada replied, "Comfort is made up of two words – 'come' and 'fort'. A 'fort' is a place of refuge. So, if we 'come' and seek 'refuge' at the Lotus Feet of the Lord, we will always be comfortable."

Dada's reply left them speechless, but also assured them that their rare and extraordinary patient was in 'comfort'.

Dada bestowed on all, his blessed and beautiful smile before being wheeled in for the surgery. His countenance, at every stage, has only reflected calm and peace. Never has a shadow of doubt, sorrow, frustration or despair ever crossed his face. It is unbelievable, at times how such a blow has befallen a body that is so delicate, tender and frail! The intensity of the pain suffered has been astronomical, far greater than regular levels of suffering, and yet Dada continued to smile and thank God, the doctors, the nurses and all those who came in contact with him.

Every day, there is a different Mantra *of gratitude on his lips. On one day it is 'Thank You, God'. On another it is* Hare Ram. *Or at times it is Satnaam Mushkul Aasaan. He holds on to these as to the Shepherd's Staff for support, never once complaining or expressing his pain. It makes one wonder at the mettle that our Guru is made of! But it is also unbearable to watch him go through this fire of suffering.*

Fortunately, Dada emerged from the recovery room, with a smile still visible on his face, providing everyone with the much needed assurance.

After the success of the procedure done on Dada's right elbow on Monday, May 17, everyone was filled with relief and gratitude. But we did not have much time to sit back and feel complacent, for God's ways are mysterious and incomprehensible. He had us on our toes immediately with the information which the doctors passed on to us, that there seemed to be no movement on the left side of Dada's body.

This alarmed the doctors and had every one of us in shock. Dada's left side would not respond to any touch or movement. After various tests and several discussions, the doctors diagnosed the problem as a mild stroke which had affected the left side of Dada's body.

Word went round the globe and prayers and chants for Dada's recovery began immediately.

To say that Dada's condition that day caused a great deal of concern to his doctors as well as his devotees – would be an understatement to the nth degree. The devotees who were with him were devastated by this unexpected blow. To most of them it seemed even worse than the original accident that had occurred just ten days ago! It seemed years had passed since that dreaded hour. There had been very many frightening and fragile moments, when it had been unbearable to watch Dada in acute pain and distress. Even his limited movements would now be restricted!

But it was only we who were devastated. Dada's radiant smile never left his face.

The smile brought tears to our eyes! How much more pain could he take?

_____

CHAPTER

4

Being True To The Guru's Teachings –
In Letter And Spirit

The *Gurbani* tells us:

Do those deeds which the Guru has ordained.
Why are you chasing after the Guru's actions?
Says Nanak, through the Guru's Teachings,
merge in the True Lord.

———

The "Third Eye", the Inner Eye of the Spirit remains closed for most of us, its vision impaired by our bad karma. The contract of the ego, the veils of arrogance and pride, have covered this inner eye completely. The Guru is the 'eye' surgeon, who can restore our inner vision.

-*J. P. Vaswani*

———

There is a great and subtle truth embodied in these lines: the truth is that we lack true maturity and wisdom to understand the actions of the Guru. It is pointless, nay, outright presumptuous to wonder why this or that came to pass; or why Dada allowed this to happen to himself. That this has happened, was not only God's Will, but also Dada's utter obedience to that Will; he allowed this accident to happen because we need to learn to be true to his teachings.

There is a reiteration of this deep truth in the *Japji Sahib* too:

> Pain is the poison. The Lord's Name is the antidote. One who sings the Glorious Praises of the True Lord, merges in the True Lord. The *Shabad* is the Guru's Gift. It shall bring you lasting peace deep within; it shall always stand by you. O *Pandit*, O religious scholar, reflect on this in your mind. Why do you read so many other things, and carry such a heavy load? Those who follow the Guru's Teachings are the true spiritual warriors.

What does Dada teach us again and again?

Qabool, qabool, qabool!
I accept, I accept, I accept!

The irony here is that he has accepted the pain and suffering, and we are reluctant to follow his example. We are still asking why and how and when and wherefore...

> Thou know'st everything, Beloved,
> Let Thy Will always be done!
> In joy and sorrow, my Beloved,
> Let Thy Will always be done!

Dada's life continues to bear witness to this utterance.

Does it not make you ask yourself: what must I do for your sake Dada? What must I do for all that you have undergone for our sake?

Let us make no mistake; saints do not suffer for no reason. When Dada went through painful physiotherapy following his second operation and even after the subsequent unexpected stroke, he would say: "Thank You God for giving me this beautiful gift. I, myself, have asked You for this gift of bestowing upon me the pain of others, so that they may suffer less. Hence, I gladly accept all this pain."

How much is there that we need to learn from Dada! Cowards like us wilt under the least strain, and yet our dearest Dada is showing us that through such tremendous pain and suffering, what our attitude should be! As we read Dada's words, let us say to ourselves, "Lord, help to let these words sink in; help me understand them and absorb them."

And once the significance of the beautiful words has sunk in, let us cry out to God: "We have understood! We have understood and absorbed the lesson! Please alleviate Dada's pain, and help us imbibe the spirit of undying faith and constant gratitude to Thee."

Let us begin putting into practice the prayer that Dada himself has taught us: the prayer of affirmation. Every time we become anxious, Dada has explained, we must

The Guru, Sadhu Vaswani taught us, is much more than an 'instructor' or 'advisor'. He is a dynamic person with a transforming power – for spirituality is a tremendous shakti; and the true Guru is a man of shakti. By the method of evocation, the Guru draws out the disciple's spiritual energy. Therefore we read in the ancient texts: "The Guru leads forth the pupil to Himself!" It is in this process of 'leading forth', drawing the disciple to Himself – not in merely communicating information – lies the secret of the Guru's shakti.

-J. P. Vaswani

repeat this prayer of affirmation with complete faith and devotion; let us do it for Dada in full faith now: "My Lord, God! Our dearest Dada is under Your Divine protection. We have no fear for him. We have cast out all fear, for we have put our Dada's good health and safety and well being into Your safe hands. Wherever Dada is, we know You will take care of him at every step, every round of life. Please accept our gratitude for protecting our Rev. Dada."

And we can follow this up right now, with Dada's prayer of universal thanksgiving:

"Thank You God! Thank You God! Thank You, God, for taking care of our Dada. Thank You, God, for healing him and making him whole again. Thank You, God, for being our support and stay!"

Not only will this send positive healing vibrations to Dada, it will transform our fears and negativities to feelings of faith and hope and joyful acceptance.

Memorable Moments With Dada

One day, Dada narrated the story of the ascetic who had lived a life of penance and *tapasya* for forty long years, seated on a grass mound atop a lonely hill, far away from all human habitation and contact.

When he gave up his physical body and went to the gates of the heaven world, he was asked by the angels: Do you want *Adul* or *Fazul?* (judgement or mercy).

He thought for a minute: he said to himself, "Why should I beg for mercy? I have lived a blameless life. I have never ever harmed anyone. I have never ever used anyone for my own selfish purposes. I have stayed away from all sin and selfish actions. So let my own worth be taken into due consideration. I do not want *fazul.* Let me be judged."

Aloud, he said to them, "I want *adul.*"

They asked him again. Again he said, "I want *adul.*"

When they asked him the same question for the third time, he lost his temper. "I have told you twice already, that I want

> When he gave up his physical body and went to the gates of the heaven world, he was asked by the angels: Do you want *Adul* or *Fazul?*

no *fazul!* I wish to be judged on my own account, which is perfectly blameless. Is it not sufficient? How many more times will you ask me?

"Alright," said the angels. "You may take your *adul.*"

Instantly, a huge form appeared before him. "Right then, I shall now sit on you," it said to him. "For forty years, you sat on me, and now it is my turn to settle accounts. I am the spirit of the hill on which you lived. Now, I shall sit on you for 40 years, then our accounts will be settled."

As you may imagine, the poor man was crushed. He cried, "Save me, please save me, I want mercy, mercy."

That was not all. Hundreds of tiny forms appeared before him, and claimed their right to eat him up. "For forty years, he made free with us, eating dozens and dozens of mountain berries and fruits. Now, it is our turn to feed on him."

Devastated, the ascetic realised that he had not lived such a free and fair life as he had fondly imagined.

So in the world in which we live, in the kinds of lifestyle that we follow, without *rahim*, without *fazul*, we are nothing!

Rahim is mercy, *Adul* is judgement. None of us can stand up to divine judgement. What we need above all else, is Divine Mercy.

For forty years the ascetic had lived a life of austerity and penance. He thought

> In the world in which we live, in the kinds of lifestyle that we follow, without **rahim**, without **fazul**, we are nothing.

he had lived a blameless life. But he had unwittingly offended the spirit of the hill and the berries which grew there. Now, when he wanted to settle his accounts, they wanted to be paid back in his own coin!

Which of us can say that he is sin-free? Even the most holy one amongst us cannot claim that he can abide by divine judgement.

In fact the more we grow in the spirit of devotion and goodness, the more the realisation will dawn on us, that we should be more merciful, more kind to all. And the more we will grow in the awareness that what we need most is God's grace and mercy.

We think we are leading blameless lives. But the seeds of sin are there within us. Therefore, we dare not ask God to judge us, to settle our accounts. We are better off, praying to Him for His infinite Mercy.

Which of us can say that he is sin-free? Even the most holy one amongst us cannot claim that he can abide by divine judgement.

A DIARY OF EVENTS

May 19-26
2010

CHICAGO

MAY 19

Between Monday evening and the following Sunday, the progress was painfully slow; but Dada's attitude helped us pass through this traumatic week with dry eyes and unshed tears firmly held back. Dada's fortitude and endurance were unbelievable, and some of it rubbed off on those who were with him!

Physiotherapy and occupational therapy are practised with Dada every day. Not only is Rev. Dada very co-operative at such times, but actually enjoys the process of therapy, and asks them for more. With Dada's ever-willing and upbeat attitude, the therapists remarked that the day's therapy is akin to a cheerleading session!

Rev. Dada has been moved to the Physiotherapy Unit of the hospital for rehabilitation. Here, his daily programme involves tremendous effort in participating in the Physiotherapy and Occupational Therapy.

Considering the mountainous hurdles that Dada has overcome so far, he is, by God's grace, doing reasonably well. There is still, of course, a lot of pain and though he is unable to move around much, Dada is not at all inactive or indolent, nor is he depressed or dejected. In fact, fully alert and aware, he pours in all his energy, will-power, patience and perseverance in attempting to physically return to normalcy as soon as possible.

In fact, on seeing Dada, the therapists exclaim, 'the Smiling One' has come. It is indeed, awe-inspiring to see that Dada's smile has not left his face even for a second since his fall.

Several devotees have questioned Dada, if Karma binds a saint. Responding to this, Dada clarified that Karma does not bind a saint, but a saint may willingly pay off the Karma of himself and of his devotees. Dada suggested that we should be very careful of what we sow. If there is any thought of ill-will or harm to another, we should immediately replace it with a good thought, and thus get rid of any negativity. In this manner, bad karma will be replaced by good karma. Dada added that just as a candle cannot be lit without fire, similarly man cannot exist without God. Just as the flame of a candle cannot survive without oxygen, so too, man cannot live without satsang.

Life in the hospital these last two weeks has confirmed for the devotees what each one of them had always believed: Dada takes the satsang with him wherever he goes. Simply to be in his presence, is to be showered by grace and blessings and is to witness the light!

CHAPTER

5

Why Did It Have To Happen?

Every occurrence, great and small, is a parable whereby God speaks to us, and the art of life is to receive and practise the message.

Rev. Dada tells us: "Our journey through this life has been perfectly planned by God's infinite love and wisdom: there can be no mistake in His plan! Every experience that comes to us is just the right one occurring at the right time to teach us the right lesson and to help us evolve in the right way. So let us accept all that comes and never attempt to circumvent anything."

Future events and happenings are concealed from us by a Loving Providence. Why probe into what God wishes to hide from us? To do so is to invite suffering. Let us trust without seeing and live without trying to unveil that which is hidden from our sight.

-J.P. Vaswani

Rev. Dada bears witness to his beliefs and ideals even in the most trying and most excruciating of ordeals!

None of us have forgotten the critical quadruple by-pass surgery he underwent in 1998! Even today, we find it too painful to recall those testing times. But during that time too, Dada summed up his experience as blithely as an angel: "I was not by-passed, I was sky-passed!"

———

Everything that happens, works for our own good. Incidents and accidents, seeming injustice, the cruelty of others, and their selfish disregard of values we hold dear – all, all of these can be seen to be the result of God's infinite goodness and unfailing love.

-J.P. Vaswani

———

It is the nature of lesser mortals like us to try and run away from all suffering and unpleasant experiences. "I wish, I would disappear!" we moan. "I wish I could just run away from it all!"

Such painful experiences, Dada has taught us, are essential to our spiritual growth. God wants us to face them and grow in moral and spiritual strength. The best way to face such difficult situations, he tells us, is not merely to accept them, but cooperate with their inner purpose, fixing our minds and hearts – not on the pain and difficulties we face – but on Him who has planned it all for us.

Suffering, Dada tells us, is of two types: the first is unnecessary suffering, which we create for ourselves through wrong thinking and wrong feeling. The second type of suffering comes to us from God: it comes to the best of men, the noblest of souls. It came to Krishna and Christ, to Buddha and Zoroaster, to Moses and Prophet Mohammed, to Nanak and Kabir, to Ramakrishna Paramahansa and Sadhu Vaswani. This type of suffering does not come alone; it brings with itself the strength, which endures, the comfort which lends sweetness to the suffering.

The suffering which man brings on himself, is hard and unbearable. (Most of us will realise that this is how we felt when we have passed through trials.) When we do not respond to life's incidents and accidents in the right attitude, it can break our spirit and throw us in an abyss of gloom.

But if we are able to cast all thoughts of self aside, and behold the loving hand of God in every condition and circumstance of life, we have a positive answer to the question: why did this have to happen?

We realise that everything that happens, happens for our good. Everything that comes to pass is the result of God's infinite goodness and unfailing love for us!

How does Dada manage to bear so much pain and keep his smile?

When we take things personally, selfishly, when we feel that we are the victims of God's unfair, unjust ways, even a little pain becomes hard to bear. But when we accept pain and suffering as God's Will for us, He takes up our burden, and the yoke becomes easy to bear!

Undoubtedly, this is what is happening to our Beloved Dada. It was he who told us words of the German mystic, Meister Eckhart: "Believe me, if there was a man who was willing to suffer on account of God and God alone, then though he fell a sudden prey to all the collective sufferings of the world, it would not trouble nor bow him down, for God would be the bearer of his burden."

And then again, we must remind ourselves of the great truth which Rev. Dada holds to be the first commandment of the Gita: You are not the body you wear; you are the immortal spirit within! Identification with the body intensifies pain and affliction. The greatest illusion to which man is bound, Dada emphasises, is identification with the body. When a great saint like Dada suffers pain, he transcends both body and mind. For such a one, there is no suffering at all!

Can we learn this lesson of transcendence? Can we overcome this constant identification with the body? Can we conquer the senses? Then we too will find that the mind can convert pain into joy and suffering into a source of peace.

Memorable
Moments With Dada

The devotees around Dada often questioned him about *karma;* how can we expiate our *karma*? Can the load of *karma* we carry ever be annihilated completely? How long – and how many more *janmas* we would require, before our *karmic* accounts were settled?

Dada explained to them again and again, that the law of *karma* is too subtle and too profound for us to comprehend it with the help of reason alone. Therefore we use comparisons like action and reaction, reaping and sowing, etc. that we may grasp its implications.

In order to understand this balance of cosmic justice, Dada told them that it is necessary for us to grasp three different aspects – three different types of *karma*:

> How can we expiate our ***karma***? Can the load of ***karma*** we carry ever be annihilated completely?

1. The first type of *karma* is *kriyaman* or *agami karma*. This is the *karma* of action and instant reaction. For example, you are thirsty and you drink water: drinking water is an effort, an action. It produces an effect immediately: your thirst is quenched. The reaction cancels out the action and the *karma* is settled, on the spot; there is no residue to be carried over. *Kriyaman karma* is that which cancels itself there and then. You take a bath; it is an action by which your body is cleansed; this is the effect

which is immediately achieved. Causes subside, when the effect is produced. Action comes to an end, when the reaction sets in. Thus, *kriyaman karma* is not carried forward. Any action of yours that leads to immediate result is *kriyaman karma*. Action and reaction – *kriya* and *pratikriya* are both completed; they have no effect on your future actions.

Those of us who have been given the gift of human birth, we may be sure that this is the result of very good *karma*.

2. The second is *sanchita karma*, the sum total and store of all our actions, good and bad, in the sequence of innumerable lives that we have lived. All of this is recorded and preserved. It is God's grace that He doesn't ask us to work out all our *sanchita karma* in one lifetime. He takes only a fragment of it that we should expiate in one lifetime. Otherwise we would be crushed beneath the weight of our own deeds!

3. The third type of *karma* is that part of our *karma* which matures, comes to fruition in one particular birth. This is *prarabdha karma* – and it is this *karma* which is the basis of our present birth, our present embodiment. Those of us who have been given the gift of human birth, we may be sure that this is the result of very good *karma*. Thus *prarabdha karma* on which our present existence is based, is often referred to as fate, destiny or luck, in popular language.

Prarabdha karma is a part, or a fragment of *sanchita karma* which has fructified in this birth. Our *sanchita karma*, accumulated over hundreds of births, is like a mountain; and in each *janma*, we are adding to the store. Of this vast store, the *prarabdha* – the inevitable – is but a fragment. It is that portion of our *karma* assigned to us to be worked out in our present existence. It is also called ripe *karma*, for it is a debt which has become overdue, and must be paid back.

Everyone grew silent and thoughtful, as the implications began to sink in.

"Can we ever annihilate all this accumulated weight of *karma*?" someone asked, after a period of silent reflection.

"Yes," Dada answered, "by complete surrender to God. Through utter self-annihilation, out of which we may attain self-realisation. This is the realisation that you are not the body that you wear, but the immortal spirit within. *Aham Brahmasmi* – when we attain this awareness everything is closed. All our *karmic* accounts are settled."

Aham Brahmasmi– when we attain this awareness everything is closed. All our *karmic* accounts are settled.

Dada then narrated the story of Ajamila from the Bhagavad Purana. Ajamila was a sinner and a wastrel, who had broken every aspect of the moral code; he had cheated, lied, looted other people's wealth, abandoned his wife and children, and lived in sin with his concubine. But at the hour of his death, when Lord Yama's messengers came to drag him to hell, he was terrified of what lay ahead; quite involuntarily, he uttered the name of Lord Narayana, aloud. Lord Yama's messengers halted in their tracks; they could not touch anyone who had uttered the name of the Lord of Vaikunth. Thus, the grace inherent in the Name Divine, was enough to annihilate Ajamila's bad *karma*, and take him to the heaven-world.

A DIARY OF EVENTS

May 26-June 3
2010

— CHICAGO —

One day, a therapist told Dada, "You look like a young man." Dada smilingly corrected him, "I am a young man."

A doctor named Dr. Harvey West came to check on Dada. On hearing his name Dada said, "You are from the West and I am from the East, and it is here that we have met. It is the need of the hour for the East and the West to come together for the beginning of a new civilisation."

Once a therapist inquired of Dada if he was tired. Dada replied, "I never get tired as long as there are three things I can do – pray without sleeping, smile all the while and serve as many as I can."

For a couple of days, Dada had a slight fever. **Dr. Ramesh Chhablani** *left no stone unturned to see that Dada received the best care. Now, by God's grace, Dada's temperature* *is back to normal and Dada is progressing as per the doctors' expectations.*

Dada often enquires about his devotees and well-wishers all over the world. He is extremely grateful to each one for the prayers and love sent to him, which have provided him with strength and helped bring about this stage of recovery. Dada continues to be extremely alert and passes on his blessings and teachings to all those he comes in contact with.

Dada narrated a beautiful story about an elderly carpenter who had worked hard all his life. He was a sincere and dedicated worker, and an asset to his employer. As he grew old and began to lose his stamina, he approached his employer and requested that, considering his age, he should be allowed to retire, although he would of course miss his regular paycheck.

The boss reluctantly agreed but requested him to work on just one more project – a new house which the boss wanted built especially, before he allowed his faithful employee to retire. The carpenter was not at all keen to take up the work and very unwillingly complied with his request. The result was that the work on the new house was hasty, half-hearted, and indifferent. On the completion of the work, he handed over the key of the house to the boss.

The employer returned the key to him, saying, "This house is meant for you as a reward for all your years of sincere and continuous hard work for me."

The carpenter was shocked and dismayed, for if he had known that the house was to be his own, he would have put in his best efforts!

Aren't we too like the carpenter? Each day, through our thoughts, words and actions, we are building the house of our lives. Each day, with our desires and cravings, we are hammering in a nail, building a wall, laying down a tile for this edifice. It is up to each one of us to make the best of our lives; let us make sure that we are later not sorry and regretful like the carpenter!

CHAPTER

6

Suffering And Pain: The Witness Of The Great Ones

It was said of Jesus, when He suffered intense pain and agony on the cross: "He came to save others; how is it that He cannot save Himself?"

That remark was obviously made in ignorance; for suffering is a gift consciously chosen and willingly accepted by saviours and saints, helpers and healers of humanity.

As Gurudev Sadhu Vaswani put it so beautifully: "Suffering is the benediction which God pours upon His beloved children to whom He would reveal the meaning of His Infinite mercy – reveal Himself, His wisdom and His love!"

———

Saints and holy men receive the arrows of pain as gifts from the all-giver. Alike in sunshine and in rain, they rejoice, give gratitude to God and sing His Holy Name. Every great one of humanity has had to bear his cross.

-J.P. Vaswani

———

It is said that when the Sufi mystic Rabia was in great affliction, one of her friends urged her to ask God for relief from pain. Rabia's answer was significant: she said to him, "Do you not know who it is that wills

How to Embrace Pain

this suffering for me? Is it not God who wills it? Why then do you bid me ask for something that is contrary to His Will? It is not well to oppose one's beloved."

The English writer, Lord Houghton, captures one such incident from Rabia's life beautifully in verse:

Round holy Rabia's suffering bed
The wise men gathered, gazing gravely-
'Daughter of God!' the youngest said,
'Endure thy Father's chastening bravely;
They who have steeped their souls in prayer
Can every anguish calmly bear.'
She answered not, and turned aside,
Though not reproachfully nor sadly;
'Daughter of God!' the eldest cried,
'Sustain thy Father's chastening gladly;
They who have learnt to pray aright,
From pain's dark well draw up delight.'
Then she spoke out, 'Your words are fair;
But, oh! the truth lies deeper still;
I know not, when absorbed in prayer,
Pleasure or pain, or good or ill;
They who God's face can understand
Feel not the motions of His hand.'

In a passage of unsurpassed beauty, Shah Abdul Latif, the beloved poet of Sind, exclaims: "I have known of no one who met the Beloved in happiness!" As

Rev. Dada himself puts it, "The Law of Love is the Law of the Cross, the Law of Sacrifice."

There is a little known story about Kunti, told to us in our ancient books: Once Sri Krishna granted her a boon to ask for whatever she wanted. What she wanted was indeed strange! She said to the Lord, "Lord, give me a little suffering all the time. For I have come to realise that in pleasures and enjoyments, You are often forgotten. But in pain and suffering, You are always remembered."

The first Sufi saints were called "those who always weep" and "those who see this world as a hut of sorrows." "Little food, little talk, little sleep," was a popular proverb amongst them. Mortification of the flesh, self denial, poverty and abstinence were seen as the means of drawing near to God, and this included fasting and long nights of prayer. The Sufis saw all suffering and pain as a means of drawing closer to God, their Beloved.

We know that Sri Ramakrishna Paramahansa, during his final days, was afflicted with acute pain and suffering due to cancer of the throat. Despite the severe pain and inability to talk, he constantly spoke to his devotees of God and spirituality. He could eat very little; but his joy and radiance were infectious. During these days of affliction, some of his devotees, unable to see his suffering due to the advanced stage of the throat cancer, begged him to cure himself through the power of prayer. The saint agreed to do this, smiling gently. But sometime later, he sent word for Swami Vivekananda and told him that he had indeed asked Mother Kali to help him overcome his inability to swallow food; but, he said to his dear devoted disciple, that the Divine Mother drew his attention to all the people in the *ashram* and in the outside world, and asked him if he was not eating through all their mouths!

When we bleed and are in pain, let us remember that the Will of God is working through us: and through suffering and pain, God's will is purifying us, preparing for the Vision of Light!

-J.P. Vaswani

The truth is that Sri Ramakrishna's consciousness was no longer tethered to the shell of his own physical body. He had transcended the physical aspect of pain and suffering.

A holy woman tells us that the Lord appeared to her, one day, and said: "I bring to you three gifts; choose the one you like the most!"

The three gifts were – undeserved criticism, disease and persecution.

The saint weighed the three gifts and found that each was more difficult to accept than the remaining two. "To be criticised for no fault of mine! To be called a bad character, a thief, a liar, a hypocrite, when I am actually innocent . . .? To become a victim to a disease, to lie in bed, unable to move, unable to get up, perhaps unable to speak, and be in this condition month after month, year after year . . .? To be treated as a criminal when my life is spotless, to be persecuted, flogged, terribly tortured . . .?"

All the three seemed unbearable, and she trembled as she thought of what would happen if she chose any of the three gifts.

The Lord smiled and, in His extended hand, were the three gifts. As she looked up into his tender, smiling face, something happened to her and, unhesitatingly she said, "Lord, I take all the three!"

A holy man who, for many years, was active in the service of God and His suffering children, said with candid simplicity: "Lord, You have cheated me! When I offered myself to Your service, I felt that all I would receive would be tears, hunger, starvation, perspiration, vexation, oppression, persecution, pain.

But You have given me the sweetest comfort. I feel cheated, Lord! But it is a happy misunderstanding."

Those that offer themselves to the service of God are out for many surprises. Their life is truly a life of adventure. Kagawa lay in hospital, threatened with total blindness. He spent many months in a dark room with thick bandages covering his eyes. When they said to him: "Your health is gone, your sight is gone. Are you not afraid of approaching death?" he calmly answered that there was nothing he feared in this wide, wonderful, God-filled world.

"As I lie in this dark room," he said, "God still gives light. Pains that pierce the very fires of Hell itself sweep over me. Yet, even in the melting fires of Hell, God's mercy, for which all of earth's manifold treasures would be an utterly inadequate exchange, still enfolds me."

"To me all things are vocal," he continued. "Oh, wonderful words of love! The bedding, the tears, the spittle, the perspiration, the vapour of the compress on my eyes, the ceiling, the matted floor, the voice of the chirping sparrow without, all are vocal. God and every inanimate thing speak to me. Thus even in the dark I feel no sense of loneliness."

Closest to our hearts, and most profoundly moving, is the account of the pain and suffering that Gurudev Sadhu Vaswani went through. It was witnessed in person and related to us by Dada, who was the Master's constant companion. Let us recall this moving account in Rev. Dada's own words:

"Gurudev Sadhu Vaswani lay ill and in great pain. He had passed a restless night: and though his eyelids were heavy with sleep, the shooting pains all over his body would not let him sleep for over a minute or two at a time. I had watched him throughout the night and had seen how even when the pain was acute, he continued to smile. When the pain became unbearable, out of his parted lips came one word: *"Shukur! Shukur!* Gratitude to Thee, O Lord of Mercy!"

His feeble body was so broken with illness and pain that it was a wonder how he could bear it. I, also, wondered that this prince amongst men, this man of singular purity and prayer, service and sacrifice, who would not hurt an ant, and who gave the love of his gentle, generous heart to all – the rich and the poor, the young and the old, the sinner and the saint, – and who loved birds and animals and every flower of the field and every lotus in the lake and every atom of matter and every ray of light – I

How to Embrace Pain

wondered that such a man should have to suffer so terribly.

Through Gurudev Sadhu Vaswani, healing had flowed to many who were sick and afflicted. Now, when he was in the throes of pain, nothing could be done to give him relief! The doctors were helpless. We, who were near him, could only wake and watch and shed hidden tears of sorrow. But all the while he rejoiced in his heart that, by making him endure great agony of body, God was using him to heal others. I recalled how it was said of Jesus in the long ago: "He saved others: Himself He cannot save!" Such is the way of those who would be the saviours and servers, the helpers and healers of Humanity!

At about three o'clock in the morning, finding it difficult to bear the sight of his suffering, I said to him: "Beloved! You are a friend of God. Why will you not pray to Him that He may heal you of this illness which your feeble body is unable to bear? Surely God will listen to your prayers!"

Quietly, he answered: "To me, my child, there is nothing sweeter than the Will of the Lord. And if it be His Will that I suffer, such suffering is sweeter to me than relief from pain: for, verily, in the fulfillment of His Holy Will is my real comfort and solace!"

After a brief while, with uplifted eyes, he prayed: "Gratitude to Thee, my God and my Lord, for this gift of pain. And if it be Thy Will to add to it tenfold, I pray Thee to do so without delay. In Thy Will alone is the peace I seek!"

And the Master added: "I know not much. I only know that there is suffering in the world. And men and women wander in the darkness. In such a world let me go about giving love and compassion to all. Let me serve the poor and broken ones, serve my brothers and sisters, serve birds and beasts and all creatures in whom is the One breath of life. Let me not waste energy in questions or controversies. Let me light a few candles at the altar of suffering creation."

We once asked Dada, "What is it that gives the saints their healing power? How do these men of God become redeemers of their race?"

Dada replied: "This, that they receive the arrows of pain as gifts from the All-Giver! Alike in sunshine and in rain, they rejoice, give gratitude to God, and sing His Holy Name. Every great one of humanity has had to bear his cross. Krishna, Buddha and Jesus walked through the valley of the shadow of death. Who are we to say, 'We must escape sorrow, anguish, pain'? We too must bear our cross, bear and bleed…

"And when we bleed, let us remember that the Will of God is working through us; and through suffering and pain, God's Will is purifying us, preparing us for the vision of the One Lord of Light and Life and Love… in all that is around us, above us, below us and within us!"

We may recall the words of St. Therese of Lisieux: "Suffering is the very best gift God can give us. He gives it only to His chosen friends."

Memorable Moments With Dada

Again and again, in Rush Medical Centre, Chicago, the devotees around Dada kept coming back to the same questions: why do saints suffer? Can *karma* really bind a saint?

Dada explained that saints often take on their sufferings gladly: one reason for this is that they wish to settle all their *karmic* accounts, and become liberated from the cycle of death and rebirth. The second is that they are profoundly compassionate by nature, and so they take on the pain and suffering of others. For them, bodily suffering has no significance. They do suffer, but once it is past, they do not even retain a memory of it. Thus it was that Sri Ramana Maharishi, Sri Ramakrishna and Sadhu Vaswani, underwent a great deal of pain and suffering in their last years...

"Do they actually feel all that pain, or do they simply transcend their suffering?" someone wanted to know.

Dada smiled. "Pain is real and actual, for everyone," he said. "Some of the saints actually suffer far more than the rest, because their bodies are very sensitive and their consciousness is profound. Gurudev Sadhu Vaswani too,

Pain is real and actual, for everyone," he said. "Some of the saints actually suffer far more than the rest, because their bodies are very sensitive and their consciousness is profound.

How to Embrace Pain

suffered on account of the slightest movements and gestures, which perhaps, we would hardly be aware of. Many of us believed that he actually took on the sufferings of others."

"It is tough and demanding to be a saint, or a holy person, is it not, Dada? And how many of us realise or appreciate the fact that a saint is taking on our suffering? Many of us simply live in ignorance, don't we? Who would want to be holy, if there is so much pain involved?"

Dada smiled and said, "Saints know the value of pain."

For the last two years of his life, Sri Ramana Maharshi suffered from cancer and experienced great physical pain, but even towards the end he maintained the same tranquil poise and the selfsame radiant smile. When he was suffering from cancer in the arm, we are told that one of his disciples ran away crying because he could not bear to see his master in pain. The Maharishi only smiled and spoke to a disciple nearby.

"Duraswami is crying because he thinks I am suffering agonies! My body is suffering but I am not suffering. When will he realise that I am not this body?"

June 4
2010

— CHICAGO —

JUNE 4

Dada's physiotherapist, Caroline, told Dada that her team would help him to get back on his feet in no time. To which Dada said, "This life is a gift from God to man. We must not try to impose our will on God. We must accept every incident and accident of life as prasad from the spotless hands of God, then we will always be happy."

Dada has, so far, undergone pain and suffering which has surpassed the agony of walking over a bed of hot coals, or climbing up a steep mountain, or lying on a bed of ice. Now, he has to further travel the road to recovery, which is also going to be difficult, uphill and arduous. We may be anxious and worried about him; but Dada, with his faith and devotion, diligence and determination, patience and perseverance, continues to tread this path successfully.

And so, Dada keeps up with his therapy. It is a long road, but he never complains. If we wish to help him in his tireless endeavour, this is what we can do: let us all, together, for ten minutes daily, do some positive visualising, seeing Dada up and about, walking at his usual brisk pace, talking to us, sitting in our midst, blessing us, guiding us, travelling energetically from one place to another and continuing to give his enriching and enlightening discourses!

A great sage has said, Prayer elevates and purifies the mind. It is associated with praise of God. It keeps the mind in tune with God. Prayer can reach a realm where reason, doubt and scepticism dare not enter. Prayer can work miracles. It makes the devotee feel nearer to God. It makes him feel the divine presence everywhere. Prayer awakens the divine consciousness in him and makes him feel his essential, immortal and blissful nature. Prayer has a tremendous influence. If the prayer is sincere and is from the depths of your heart, it will at once melt the heart of the Lord.

So, let all of us, around the globe, send forth such deep and sincere prayers which will surely 'melt the heart' of our Lord, making the quick and complete recovery of our beloved Dada, as part of His Will and His Plan.

CHAPTER

7

What We
Need to
Learn?

One of Dada's bestselling books titled **Why Do Good People Suffer?** has gone through multiple editions, and people who have read the book on their own accord, or received it from their friends in times of personal crisis, vouch that it has endowed them with stability and strength when they have faced seemingly insurmountable problems.

The best way to tackle suffering and pain, according to Dada, is presented below:

1. We must take our mind away from the thought of suffering. If our attention is focused on suffering, it tends to get multiplied manifold.

2. In times of pain and suffering, we must learn to count our blessings. For those of us who are so pessimistic as to imagine that there are no blessings to count, there is a simple exercise. We can take a piece of paper and list all the things in our life which we have been blessed with.

3. We must learn to dissociate ourselves from the body, the mind and the ego. This is not easy, but it is the first step towards self-realisation. It is the mind that creates all our suffering; once we transcend the mind, there is no suffering at all – only peace and joy.

How to Embrace Pain

4. In all conditions and circumstances of life, we must continue to thank the Lord. We must make it a habit, to praise the Lord at every step, in every round of life. Even in the midst of fear and frustration, worry and anxiety, depression and disappointment, let the words, "Thank You God! Thank You God! Thank You God!" be on our lips constantly. We will find that we are filled with a sense of peace.

The best way to face the ups and downs of life is to accept them and cooperate with their inner purpose, all the while fixing our mind and heart on Him who has planned for each one of us the glorious liberty that belongs to children of the spirit.

-J.P. Vaswani

---

5. Do not try to run away from trouble and pain. They are essential to our growth. God means us to face them with courage and acquire strength and wisdom.

6. Accept the Will of the Lord and fix your minds and hearts on God. Realise that God is always by our side, watching us, guiding us, guarding us and protecting us.

Through Dada's pain and suffering, we have come to realise that life is not a bed of roses, but a battlefield, which requires all the strength of the spirit. The strength of the spirit is far more powerful, far more important, than the strength of the body. Therefore, our ancient *rishis* called it *atma-shakti* Those who have this *atma-shakti*, are the ones who can face life with ease and grace, as Dada has practically demonstrated to us.

To move Godward, we need to get up and open the door and let God in. This happens only when man realizes the need for God. Out of the very depths of his heart, there awakens the cry, "I have need of Thee, Lord! I cannot live without Thee!"

-J.P. Vaswani

It is an accepted fact of the Hindu faith that saints can take on the *karma* of their devotees upon themselves. It is like the incidents we have heard about Gurudev Sadhu Vaswani and of Dada who often bought captive birds from a vendor, or fish caught in a fisherman's net and released them, setting them free from captivity. Dada who is immeasurably rich and powerful in the wealth of the spirit, may, if he so desires, pay for our *karma*, and help to release us from the cage of *maya*.

Let us therefore, learn the lesson well: our beloved master and mentor, is enduring physical pain, so we might learn from his example, and attempt to be better human beings and become more and more like him. As Dada often tells us, the biggest room in our lives is the room for improvement!

And we may recall Rev. Dada's words, "It is life that is needed, not doctrines, creeds or dogmas. Let us bear witness to the great teachings of the saints in deeds of daily living."

Yes, it is life that is needed, not book-learning nor psychological or intellectual interpretations. Books, doctrines, philosophical interpretations will not make us new. What we need is a new way of life, a new pattern of thinking, a new heart! And our hearts will become new when we practise all that has been taught to us, in a spirit of understanding, acceptance, faith and love for God.

Memorable Moments With Dada

The discussion one day in the hospital, revolved around the difficulty of absolute surrender to the Lord. Is it possible for us to practise it today, when surrender is equated with cowardice?

Dada smiled his radiant smile. "If people call you a coward just because you have surrendered the thread of your life into God's hands," he remarked, "well then, you must accept that criticism also in a spirit of surrender!"

Dada then narrated a little known story about Draupadi. The battle of Kurukshetra was over and the Pandavas were seated around Krishna in a tent, when Draupadi said, 'O, Lord, I have a question to ask You! You are the One who offers redemption to all who surrender unto You. Therefore, You are worshipped as *'Aapat Bhaandava'*, the Comforter in calamities. You rushed to Gajendra's call. You rushed to Prahalada's call. But, in my case, when I was ill-treated in the court of the Kauravas, I wailed and wept and shed bitter tears, before You finally appeared to rescue me. O, Gopala, what took You so long? What sin did I commit that You were so slow to answer my pleas?"

> "O, Gopala, what took You so long? What sin did I commit that You were so slow to answer my pleas?"

Sri Krishna smiled and said, "Draupadi, when Dushasana wanted to disrobe you, do you remember whom you called first? You called each of your husbands, you appealed to the elders, the great warriors in Dhritarashtra's court, and all the brave men. And then, you gathered courage, and tried to fight off Dushasana on your own. Only at the end, when all else had failed you, you turned to me for protection. You held your hands together in supplication and prayed to Me, and called on Me to come and help you. Tell Me: did I not come as soon as you called Me?"

Draupadi understood the true meaning of surrender. She had surrendered to Krishna only as a last resort. Had she surrendered to Him at the outset, her story might have been different.

"True and absolute surrender to the Lord is not easy," Dada observed. "It is a difficult path that only the chosen few can walk. The worldly path is a lot easier to tread. But will it take you where you want to go? That is the question."

Everyone present recalled Dada's teachings on the two paths before us – *preya*, the smooth, easy and wide path of pleasure; and *shreya,* the tough, rocky, hard path that was difficult to tread.

"Many people are tempted to choose the easy path, aren't they Dada? Why risk the pleasures and gains we can enjoy on this worldly path for the sake of the intangible rewards which we cannot see or understand?"

"True and absolute surrender to the Lord is not easy," Dada observed. "It is a difficult path that only the chosen few can walk"

"What is it that makes you choose the tough path, the right path? Perhaps it is the guiding hand of God, the voice of His angels, who lead you onward, Godward."

"But something is there, that also draws you back to the good, the noble and the difficult – the path of *shreya*," Dada observed. "What is it that makes you choose the tough path, the right path? Perhaps it is the guiding hand of God, the voice of His angels, who lead you onward, Godward."

A DIARY OF EVENTS

June 8
2010

CHICAGO

JUNE 8

Dada repeatedly tells us, swift-footed time has moved on; although to many of us, this month has seemed more like a yuga, time has most certainly moved on…

It is painful and heart-breaking to look back on the past month. What do we call this month? When we asked Dada about this, his answer was unbelievable. He said, "For me, it has been a Month of Mercy. I feel that God, in His infinite mercy, has chosen me to bear this cross of pain and suffering, in order to lighten the load of others and bring comfort and relief to their distressed lives."

Truer words were never spoken! Many of us recall the dark and depressing days of December, 1992, when India was being torn by communal riots, following the demolition of the Babri Masjid. Amidst the general strife and disharmony that swept the nation, Pune surprisingly remained an oasis of peace.

At that time, Dada was suffering from excruciating pain in his shoulders. So great was the pain that several of his engagements had to be cancelled, and doctors were attending on him daily to monitor his treatment and alleviate the pain.

At that time, Swami Satchitananda came to visit Dada. Watching the doctor attending to Dada, the saint inquired what the diagnosis was. The doctor explained the problem in medical parlance, but the saint shook his head and smiled. "Dada is carrying the pain of the people on his shoulders," he explained. "That is why his city Pune, is peaceful, while the rest of the country is burning."

We realise now, that this is not as far-fetched as it sounds. Throughout this Month of Mercy, as Dada has named it, we have been receiving messages from devotees around the world, who have experienced a healing, a relieving respite from their problems in different ways. A devotee in his early seventies had a major fall, but recuperated from the ensuing surgery in no time, and is mobile and back to normal. Another had developed muscle damage near the hips and had been experiencing pain for over seven months. No medication could reduce her pain. Now she is pain-free and going about her regular chores. These people are convinced that it is Dada's pain that has taken their pains away! But these and other devotees vehemently assert that they would gladly give up their new-found relief and go back to bear all the pain, if only they could but alleviate Dada's suffering, even in a miniscule degree! But as they are unable to do so, they are bowing down to His Will, gratefully acknowledging the fact that Dada's offering, his sacrifice, suffering and pain have not been in vain.

For all of us, it has been a Month of Mercy wherein we have forgotten to be selfish and obsessed with our mundane, egotistical concerns. Dada proclaimed aloud: "Hold and behold all with mercy." May this Month of Mercy teach us all to view each and every one around us with the warmth and caring of mercy. All of us have rediscovered the healing power of prayer; we have been praying and pleading with God to pour His mercy on Dada, and make him healthy and whole again.

Hopefully this month of intense prayer and yearning will have strengthened us to a point where we can focus on channelising all the positive energy towards healing our Beloved Dada.

Dada narrated a beautiful story about how Burbank demonstrated the inexplicable and intense power of love. Burbank would shower tremendous love on his roses; he would even speak love filled words to them. In his daily conversation he lovingly asked them to grow without thorns and miraculously it happened. The roses actually grew without any thorns! It is this intensity of love that we should feel for God and one another, in order to experience the true power of love.

CHAPTER

8

What We
Need To
Do?

Those of us who are fortunate enough to look upon Rev. Dada as our Guru, can vouch for this: whenever we have had to face difficult situations, Dada's words of wisdom have always provided courage and guidance for us. Some of us seek his advice directly, in person, through calls, or through letters and e-mails. Some of us receive guidance through remarks and observations that he makes in his discourses, which, miraculously, seem to offer us a practical solution to our problems. Yet others, we know, open his books, and thus find the answer they seek. The wisdom and kindness of the Guru are indeed wonderful! Like God's providence, they too work in miraculous ways!

Now, when we face this unprecedented situation of seeing our master, teacher and spiritual mentor being subjected to such severe pain and intense therapeutic procedures, when we are forced to see our beloved Dada confined to his room and unable to move about freely, to whom can we turn for comfort and consolation?

If this question has indeed crossed your mind, you can be assured that others have also felt the same. In fact, one of the brothers who was by Dada's bedside in the Rush Medical Centre at Chicago, actually placed this question before Dada, on behalf of us all. Let us report this conversation here for your benefit:

Q: Dada this is an important question, we all turn to you for help, indeed many of us actually pray to you when we have a problem. We think of you; if we are away from you, we visualise your image in our hearts, and we earnestly request you to help us. The thing is, when YOU have a problem, whom can we turn to? Many of us even route our prayers to God through your grace, and ask Him to help us because we are your children. You are everything to us Dada! But can we pray to you *for* you?

(Dada smiles…)

Absorbed as we are, in the pursuit of the shadow shapes of wealth, pleasure and power, we will do well to pause to ask ourselves the question, "What is the goal of life?" It cannot be wealth or possessions, pleasure or power, for we know we drop this body at the end of this earthly life. What then is the goal of this life? The goal is God!

-J.P. Vaswani

Q: Dearest Dada, could we do this?

Dada: Yes, yes, yes, absolutely…

Q: So now I am praying to you, make yourself good... please Master, you can do it, not for yourself, but for our sake, as our Master. Please Dada.

(Dada laughs)

That conversation should prove to be an eye-opener for us all. And, indeed, we would do well to remember that Dada has taught us, on several occasions, how to face difficulties and trials, and surmount obstacles with the help of God and the Guru!

———

We must establish more and more points of contact with God. This will give you peace and stability of the soul, and out of you, the joy of God will flow to many. Be gentle with all those who come to you. They have been sent by God to your door, not without a purpose.

-J. P. Vaswani

———

So let us offer you a recap of those practical suggestions which Dada has given us through his discourses and his inspiring books: the only difference is this, that we used these techniques in the past to solve our personal problems. Now, we shall collectively put them into practice to wish, to will with all our hearts, indeed to actualise into concrete reality our dearest, most devout hope that our beloved Dada, our dearest Master may be well, and healed and whole very soon, as we have known him and seen him and loved him and been blessed by his presence amongst us all these years!

Practical Suggestion 1: Let us hand our anxiety and care over to the Lord. In Dada's words, let us let go, let go, let God! Let God take care of our beloved Dada and make him well again. What seems insurmountable and impossible to us, is possible, indeed, effortless for God! So why are we holding on to grief and anxiety and fear? Let us discard these negative feelings at the Lotus Feet of Him who can turn the impossible to I'm possible!

Practical Suggestion 2: Let us expect the best and get it! As Dada has taught us, the power of thought is the greatest, and also the most under-utilised power in this world. If we think good thoughts, thoughts of hope and courage, love and compassion, beauty and joy, faith and freedom, of peace and harmony, we invite to ourselves good forces, forces of light; in that measure, we actually create the reality that we think of.

Practical Suggestion 3: Let us practise the power of silence. Dada has always urged us to begin the day with God, by spending a few minutes in silent communion with Him. If you practise this regularly, devote this special period of the early morning communion to send healing vibrations and prayers for Dada's speedy recovery. If, perchance, you have not really put this into practice earlier, well, it is time to start now! As a newcomer to this practice, who knows, your silent prayers may have far more impact than those of us who pray regularly!

Practical Suggestion 4: Let us conquer fear; let us drive out despair and pessimism from our hearts and lives. Now is the time to put into practice what Dada has always urged us to do. Faith is the best weapon in our spiritual armoury to drive out the demon of fear. When fear knocks at the door of our hearts, let us send our faith to open the door. We will surely find that fear vanishes as mist before the morning sun!

Practical Suggestion 5: Let us practice the power of positive visualisation. Let us picture the best; let us hope to get the best results even from the worst conditions. It is an inviolable law of life, Dada says, that when you visualise and expect good, nothing but good will come to you.

Practical Suggestion 6: Let us offer the best that we have to Dada; therefore, let us now seize every opportunity we have to serve others. When we go out of our way to help a brother here, a sister there, a tiny bird, or a wounded animal, we are offering to God the best and purest that we are capable of – i.e. selfless service. The love and service that we offer to those in need, those less fortunate than ourselves, reaches God directly and pleases Him more than our offerings of gold and silver. Let us give of ourselves; let us offer humble, loving, unconditional service to all those who need it most.

Practical Suggestion 7: Let us harness the power of prayer for our beloved Dada. As Dada tells us, prayer is not at all a difficult matter. It is simply like meeting your best friend. Let us do likewise with Him who is the Friend of all friends. All we have to do is close our eyes, shut out the world, open our hearts, and call out to Him with deep love and longing, and we will surely see Him right before us, in our heart, ready to respond to our call! He is our father, mother, our guide, our guardian and friend, all rolled into one. Let us tell Him to heal beloved Dada and make him healthy and active, as he was before. Let us make miracles happen with our powerful prayers!

When we all pray together for our beloved Dada, what is there that God will not grant us?

Memorable Moments With Dada

A Question-Answer session with Dada

Q: Dada, what is it that we can do so that you may get well soon?

Dada: First of all, prayer; secondly, selfless service; and thirdly, reading of the Scriptures.

Q : Is there any particular scripture Dada, which you could prescribe?

Dada: You can read whichever scripture is dear to you. If you wish, you can read the Sukhmani Sahib.

Q: And should we read it fully at a time?

Dada : No, that is not always necessary. Even if you read one page at a time, it is good. But you must read it with understanding. This is why in the *satsang*, we use the *Sukhmani Sahib* translated by Gurudev Sadhu Vaswani in Sindhi, where the meaning is clearly and beautifully explained. You can read a page or even one verse at a time – but you must read it with understanding and devotion.

> You can read a page or even one verse at a time – but you must read it with understanding and devotion.

Q: And what kind of seva can we take up for you, Dada?

Dada : All seva is good. There should be love in the *seva*, you must do *seva* with love and humility; that is what makes it an offering of love to the Lord.

Dada then narrated the story of Bhai Kanhaiya, the very symbol of service with love and devotion. We look upon Henry Dunant, founder of the Red Cross, as the first humanitarian who initiated the tradition of selfless service for the care of war victims, Dada remarked; but the truth was that Bhai Kanhaiya took up this activity, more than 100 years before the inception of the Red Cross.

Bhai Kanhaiya was born the son of a wealthy trader, but his heart was focused on the ideals of *seva* and *simran*. (Service and silent prayer). His special mission was selfless service of humanity with no distinction of nationality, caste or creed. Therefore, he founded a *dharmashala*, and offered food to the hungry and needy, while also conducting regular *satsangs* for the people. In 1705, he was on a visit to Anandpur, when the city was invaded by aggressors. The city was simultaneously attacked by hill tribes from Afghanistan, and put under siege by the imperial army of the Mughals. There was severe shortage of food and water, and wounded soldiers lay dying all over the city. In such difficult times, Bhai Kanhaiya used to roam around serving water to the wounded and the dying without distinction of friend and foe.

> You must do **seva** with love and humility; that is what makes it an offering of love to the Lord.

Some Sikhs complained to Guru Gobind Singh that Kanhaiya had been resuscitating the fallen enemy soldiers. "When the city is under siege, why should we give away our limited supply of water to Turks and Muslims?" they demanded to know.

Guru Gobind Singh summoned Bhai Kanhaiya and told him that complaints had been brought against him. "Is it true that you helped enemy soldiers?" the Guru asked him. "Answer this question, before your brothers who have felt aggrieved by your actions."

"Yes, my Lord," agreed the loyal Sikh. "What they said is true in a sense; but I swear to you that I saw no Mughals or Sikhs in the battlefield; I only saw the Guru's face in everyone."

> "I swear to you that I saw no Mughals or Sikhs in the battlefield; I only saw the Guru's face in everyone."

The Guru, pleased with the reply, blessed him and told his Sikhs that Kanhaiya had understood his teaching correctly. The Tenth Guru not only appreciated his benevolent act, but took out a vial of ointment and gave it to him, asking him to apply it to the wounds of the soldiers whom he served.

This is why Bhai Kanhaiya is rightly called the forerunner of the modern Red Cross. He left behind the unique movement of *Sewa Panthi*, which literally means people devoted to service of humanity.

A DIARY OF EVENTS

June 15- 25
2010

CHICAGO

JUNE 15

Dada's growing strength and improving health ensure that his progress is continuous, steady and encouraging. Dada's physiotherapist, Caroline, is extremely pleased with the improvement in his condition and works very hard at ensuring that Dada obtains the maximum support. In return, he puts in his best effort. In gratitude for her sincere efforts, Dada actually wrote a sweet poem for her.

Dada told her that he has had many teachers in his life, but she has been the best teacher for him. She replied that this was so because he has been and is still the best student, and hence, he has been her inspiration to become such a good teacher. She is aiming high and told Dada that she was looking forward to the day, when he completes his physiotherapy in Chicago, and walks all the 1000 miles to New York! Unfazed, Dada sportingly replied that he would surely do so, but on the map! Once again, he provides us with a glimpse of his ever-present sense of humour, his sparkling wit and his instantaneous presence of mind.

Dada is now staying at the Johnston R. Bowman Apartments, where a very warm welcome was extended to him by **Ms. Nancy Schaffer Lodding,** Director of Residential Services.

Dada is regularly made to play board games like scrabble, etc. This is an essential part of his occupational therapy. For instance, while playing scrabble, he has to pick up and arrange the letters. This provides excellent movement and exercise for the arms, wrists and fingers. Yet, it is fun, so the therapy does not feel like a dreary chore.

Dada's doctor, **Dr. Pang,** is extremely pleased with Dada's encouraging and steady progress. He has totally taken to Dada, and sometimes joins us in our daily satsang, even though he does not understand a word. He says he just loves the positive energy that emanates from Dada at such times. He, like all of us, is looking forward to the day when Dada, even if it be with the help of a walking stick, can walk on his own. After that he feels, Dada will be ready to proceed to New York.

Dada is not just lying in bed. His daily schedule is very stringent. His physiotherapy commences at 7 a.m. He is finally free only at 11.30 p.m. But he is doing well, so it makes all the effort worth it.

Dada gives us some impromptu upadeshes and even has brief Question & Answer

Sessions. A visitor once asked Dada for one simple rule to follow in life. Dada replied, "God is inside and outside. This knowledge should enable you to live like a child, with no worry, anxiety or fear. Everything is regulated by Him, so we should leave it all in His Hands."

While Caroline, the physiotherapist, is putting Dada through the strenuous exercises, she is constantly concerned that they should not take too much of a toll on Dada's strength and energy. So, she repeatedly asks him if everything is alright, as she proceeds with the physiotherapy. Dada always replies with a smile, "All my experiences and lessons from you are for my good, to improve my muscle tone and enable me to walk. Similarly, God too sends us experiences which are for our enrichment and good."

There is still a long and laborious journey ahead for Dada. But then every journey is traversed through earnest effortful steps and Dada's eager, baby steps will soon enable him to run, transcending all obstacles, and reaching out to all of us, thirsty souls, who yearn for his speedy recovery.

CHAPTER

Thank You, God!

How better to begin the end of this profoundly intriguing turn of events, than by referring to Dada's words:

> Count your blessings and thank God every living, waking, moment– for God's generosity to you is infinite!

Every accomplishment, every form of excellence, every success, small or big, belongs to God. If you are wise and intelligent, it is God-given. If your hard work and efforts are commendable, it is due to the grace of God. If you are truly conscious of this, and acknowledge His grace in all humility – why, this humility too is a manifestation of His mercy upon you!

When we learn to thank the Lord in prosperity and plenty, we will also grow in the realisation that we owe thanks to Him in adversity and misery as well. In the words of Gurudev Sadhu Vaswani we learn to regard every disappointment as His appointment. We realise that he upsets our plans, only to set up His own! When we learn to thank the Lord in all conditions, we will grow in the realisation that we are but instruments of His Divine Will – and is this not the most wonderful thing to be grateful for?

The last three months, the Month of Mercy, the Month of Healing and the third Month of Acceptance

Look around you for a moment.
Marvel at the vastness of the blue
sky; the splendour of the sun,
moon and stars and the magnificent
panorama of nature.
Count your blessings and thank
God, every living, waking,
moment– for God's generosity to
you is infinite!

-J.P. Vaswani

are taking us to the culminating day – August 2, 2010, Rev. Dada's 92nd Birthday, which is for all of us, not just a day of celebration, but a day of Thanksgiving. Twelve years ago, the Thanksgiving Week was instituted from February 18 to 24, to be observed every year with acts of gratitude and service offered to God for healing Rev. Dada after his critical quadruple by-pass surgery. Today, greater gratitude we owe to God, as we prepare to celebrate our beloved Guru's birthday; for God has shown us that He is always at hand, to answer our every need and every prayer. Who can deny that we will be celebrating this memorable "birthday with a difference" solely due to His infinite grace and kindness?

But we owe an equal, if not greater debt of gratitude to beloved Dada. It is he who has suffered the most, strained himself to the utmost, and put himself through a veritable trial of endurance. He has undergone a prolonged period of pain and agony – first, following the fall and triple fracture; second, during two successive major orthopedic surgical procedures; third, while suffering that cruel blow of a partial stroke, soon after the second surgery; and fourthly, bravely taking on the tough and taxing routine of rehabilitative therapy, with all its attendant pain – all for the sake of us, his undeserving children, who know only one thing: that they love him and need him above all else.

Of course it was God's Will that all of this had to happen; needless to say, not a word of complaint or distress has passed Dada's lips; we have broken our hearts and wept; we have shed tears of grief and despair; but Dada has withstood all the trauma with a smile, making even the doctors marvel at his positive, cheerful, uncomplaining attitude! What a wonderful example for us all!

Rev. Dada always says that in the U.S.A., they have one celebratory, Thanksgiving Weekend; but for all of us, true Thanksgiving cannot be confined to a single day: indeed, every day, every moment of every day should be occasions of Thanksgiving. The spirit of Thanksgiving should so infuse our life that it should transform our life into a constant remembrance of His infinite Mercy on us!

Here is a little prayer that Dada often says:

O Lord, I seek neither wealth nor power, nor the
pleasures of this or the next world.
I need Thee and Thee alone!
Grant me the gift of longing – deep yearning – for
Thy Lotus Feet!
Grant me the gift of tears – that I may keep awake at
night and meditate
And, during the day, help as many as I can,
To lift the load on the rough road of life!
I thank Thee Lord, for Thy infinite mercy to me!

True thankfulness leads us on to generous giving and
sharing. The more grateful we are, the more we are
inclined to share what we have with others. In this as
in so much else, the more we give, the more we get –
whether it is gifts, wealth, love or friendship. It is this
spirit of loving and giving, caring and sharing, that
Dada cherishes above all else; and it is this spirit of
selfless service that he would like us all to imbibe from
him. Very close to Dada's heart is the Vedic Prayer
that goes thus:

Sarve bhavantu sukinah
Sarve Santu niraamayaah
Sarve bhadraani pashyantu
Ma kaschit dukh bhaag-gavet

May all be happy, may everyone enjoy the good, may
everyone be free from the misery of ignorance, disease
and suffering! What a beautiful attitude this prayer
teaches us! If only each one of us holds this attitude

in our hearts, and sends out vibrations of goodwill and love to all around us, we are expressing the best form of thanksgiving to God!

The best way in which we can offer this prayer to the Almighty is to be true to its words in letter and spirit, by offering acts of selfless service and compassion to all living beings whose lives touch our own.

—

Offering thanks to God teaches us one of the most valuable lessons of life – to appreciate the here and now. We learn to stop wishing for what-might-have-been and yearning for what-is-not, and enjoy what is, now. So we offer thanks, we focus on the present moment, and experience the full wonder of the precious present moment.

-J.P. Vaswani

—

Let us thank God for restoring our Rev. Dada to good health. But let us go one step further. Let us thank God for the sorrow we have undergone, knowing that it has taught us to cultivate faith and trust in His goodness. Let us remember the pain that Dada has been put through, and let us imbibe the qualities of sympathy and compassion for everyone who is in pain. Let us thank God, that because of the trauma that Dada has been put through, we have been witness to his wonderful virtues of forbearance and patience. Let us thank God for all the brothers and sisters, who have been by Dada's side during this ordeal, and represented the collective devotion of us all; let us thank God for the wonderfully supportive medical team who have surrounded Dada with their healing care and protection, and helped him take those crucial steps towards recovery; let us thank **Dr. Ramesh Chhablani, Dr. Walter Virkus, Dr. Mark Cohen, Dr. Thomas Pang, Dr. Gopal Lalmalani, Ms. Caroline Saavedra, Ms. Nancy Schaffer Lodding and the entire team**; let us thank God for those millions of loving hearts, the devotees, friends and admirers whose collective good wishes and prayers have been poured on Dada like a benediction from heaven; let us thank God for the vicarious suffering we have undergone with Rev. Dada, for it has taught us courage and enduring faith. Let us thank God for the disappointments we have borne – for they have taught us to be ever ready for His appointment!

Memorable Moments With Dada

Dada's first love has always been the sea. As Chicago is far away from the coast, it was decided that the next best thing would be to take Dada to the beautiful shores of Lake Michigan. It is one of the five Great Lakes of North America, and the only one located entirely within the United States. Lake Michigan beaches are known for their beauty. The region is often referred to as the "Third Coast" of the United States, after those of the Atlantic Ocean and the Pacific Ocean.

The thought of this trip, which was going to be the first outing for Dada, after so many days of being indoors, had everyone extremely excited. Dada's therapist who was on leave that day, decided to join him on this excursion. Dr. Pang, the doctor in charge of Dada, also came along. There was a quiet sense of jubilation, as the party set out with Dada for the Lake.

It was a bright, beautiful and sunny day, with not a cloud in the electric blue sky. The water of the Lake shimmered like pure silk. The waterfront was crowded with people, all out to enjoy this beautiful summer day. Unlike the tumultuous waves of the ocean, the

> The thought of this trip, which was going to be the first outing for Dada, after so many days of being indoors, had everyone extremely excited.

ripples on the Lake were gentle and calm. It was such a pleasure to see the sun shining on Dada's face, and the wind playfully ruffling his hair. The balmy breeze was soothing and comforting and Dada continued to enjoy this entire scene through the window of his car. Unlike the rest of the group, Dada's face reflected calm and peace. He remarked that whatever the weather outside maybe, whether it was sunny or raining, hot or cold, he was always happy and full of bliss. For he believes that whatever God has planned for Him is the very best.

The lake reminded Dada of the time when Jesus gave his teaching at the historic Lake of Galilee. It was about Jesus's first meeting with His disciples. Jesus had come across some fishermen who were busy plying their trade on the lake. He told them to come unto Him, for He would teach them to become "fishers of men" and to come closer to God. They were so lucky and fortunate, Dada observed, to have come into close proximity with a saviour of Humanity. It was important in life to have a Guru, Dada added. The Guru transports us to a world of new dimensions, fragrant, fair and fresh. In comparison, this material world is dark and gloomy.

Whatever happens in our lives, Dada added, is the result of our *karma*. Its seed lies dormant within us. Sooner or later, maybe even in the next birth, it will surely sprout and grow into a tree, which will bear fruit. The fruit may be sweet or bitter, sour or tasteless, but we will have to eat it. Hence, we must not

> The Guru transports us to a world of new dimensions, fragrant, fair and fresh. In comparison, this material world is dark and gloomy.

We must not
cry or protest
or shed tears
of sorrow.
Rather, we
should let our
hearts roll out
prayers in
gratitude to
God

cry or protest or shed tears of sorrow. Rather, we should let our hearts roll out prayers in gratitude to God. "Let the *mantra* of our life be *'Shukur, Shukur'*, Thank You Lord, Thank You Lord".

A DIARY OF EVENTS

NEWS UPDATE

As we go to press with this book, which is our dedicated offering to all those who suffer and are in pain, as well as the helpers and healers who make their pain manageable, we hear that Dada's doctors in Chicago have expressed great satisfaction with the miraculous progress that Dada has made, in the last week or so. With the grace of God and the ever-present blessings of Gurudev Sadhu Vaswani, Dada will be permitted to leave the Rush Medical Centre and travel to New York on July 17, 2010.

It is the doctors' collective opinion that Dada's recovery is nothing short of miraculous.

We end with the final, happy report from Chicago, dated July 16:

The last week of Rev. Dada's stay in Chicago saw an endless flow of visitors consisting of members of the hospital staff to Dada's apartment. As the staff members of the Rush Medical Centre began to realise that Dada would be leaving the hospital soon, they began to drop in to take his blessings and wish him a speedy recovery.

The doctors who had always been regular visitors, remarked that no other 'patient' at the hospital had ever had such an impact on the staff, so much so that everyone wanted to meet him personally before he left. It must be remembered too, that thousands of patients have been treated at the hospital for longer or shorter durations, and left the hospital, year after year! But such was the effect of Dada's magnetic persona, such was the response he evoked in all the hospital staff, that they openly confessed that Dada's discharge, would leave a void in their lives and in their work environment, which he had made so vibrant with his presence. It is indeed so true that saints create a heaven wherever they go even if it maybe in the environs of sickness and suffering in a hospital. They spread the magic of their holy presence to all those around them.

It was Rev. Dada's suggestion that an informal Farewell Get Together should be held in the apartment for all his newfound friends, admirers, helpers and healers in the hospital. The food for the party was cooked and served by the brothers and sisters in the apartment kitchen. The Indian food cooked was so tasty and so popular among the visitors that they asked to take some of it back home for their families. It seemed as if the birthday celebrations had started early, and there was a langar (fellowship meal) being held at Dada's apartment!

The distinguished gathering of doctors, therapists and hospital administrators in a patient's apartment was unprecedented! Each and every one of them said that meeting Dada, treating him, and providing their services to him, had been unique and a life-

transforming experience for them. Never before in their careers had they come across a person who had touched their hearts and spirits as Dada had. The staff members received a sumptuous meal, a sweet souvenir return gift and above all the spontaneous outpouring of divine benedictions of our Dear Dada. Once again, it reminds us of the fact that no one returns empty handed from the door of a true saint… he gives and gives and only gives.

In a brief but moving address, Dada said to his guests, "Turn Back to God. Make God the central presence of your life. Depend on Him, and Him alone, for all your needs, great and small. Remember, He is just a prayer away from you."

What can we say about the exhilarating and miraculous effect that a saint has on his environment! For ten weeks, Dada had graced the Rush Medical Centre Hospital with his presence. The medical staff at the hospital had helped to heal him and put him back on its feet. And he, for his part, left the hospital, spreading around him positive vibrations and countless blessings that will long linger in their minds and hearts, like the whiff of divinely fragrant flowers!

So The Doctors Felt...

I've had the opportunity to work with Dada during his stay at Rush University Medical Center in physical therapy. Whenever he enters the clinic he always has a smile and happily raised eyebrows, despite all of the medical issues he has been through. There are many things that could make him sad, angry or unmotivated but he does not choose these things and embraces this physical challenge opportunity. It is evident right away that he is positive, trusting and diligent about getting better. These factors have been the foundation for his recovery. Dada began his therapy in the room then progressed to the clinic then progressed to walking and the stairs. I hope that Dada continues his journey of recovery by taking the tools he has learned here and applying them to his home life. Best wishes.

Thank you,

Margot McCloy, PT, DPT

"Medicine is not secular" - JP Vaswani

It was such a pleasure, compared to the day before, when I first met Dada at his sombre bed side, I asked Dada to sing for me.

He looked up and I gazed upon his ageless eyes. He replied to me: "I do not sing. But, for you I will."

After a brief pause, he began to sing the most beautiful profound lyrics. And thus I began an inspirational rehabilitation journey with Dada.

I was able to envision his course of recovery, and at the same time, I became spiritually nourished daily by Dada.

Despite the complexities of his medical status, Dada expressed humane dignity and peace, as he participated in the rigors of rehabilitation. Day by day, with our team and, now my family, devoted members, he progressed.

Soon he began his evening *satsangs* and we all bloomed once again. The ever presence of his sunshine rays of spiritual messages, always carried us along with his daily routine at the medical center.

Because I have had the privilege of working with Dada daily, I cherish his union of God's compassion, service, and gifts that allow me to be a physician, allowing me to follow Dada's heart, mind, body and spirit, as well as, all my patients before me.

He continues to help me with my predictions of his recovery. Just recently I asked Dada if he can dance. He replied that he does not. He is now learning salsa steps!

Dada is magnetic and humble, someone with whom I wish to make house calls with over and over again. His timeless smiles will stay with me and keep me spiritually aloft.

Dr. Thomas Pang, MD

When Dada Vaswani had come in April, his sight had faltered. Although we had planned on cataract surgery, my exam revealed parched corneas, and I asked, "How long have you been in pain?"

With his signature smile, he told me that for some months, he had felt soreness in his eyes. I admired his ability to travel the world, write books, and lecture with eye pain and Dr. Gopal Lalmalani said, "Dada, you are not of the body."

"But I have a body," was his reply.

These past few months, I have seen that body suffer multiple fractures, swollen, bruised, manipulated, and ultimately hang limp after a stroke. Yes indeed, he has a frail body.

But he is not of the body. Dada Vaswani has, by God's grace, with a smile and quick wit, with comfort to all around him, carried on with infectious enthusiasm. I marvel at how he can bear the pain with a smile. I am witness to a miracle.

Being in his presence through this ordeal has touched and transformed me. I try to live in joy no matter what troubles litter my path. When those troubles gather, I think of Dada's example and surprisingly find peace.

Dada Vaswani has a body, a body that has suffered a great deal these last few months. His courageous response to this has shown me that he is not of the body, he is Sat-chit-ananda.

Dr. Balaji Gupta, MD
July 13, 2010

I first met Dada when he came to JRB and the first thing I saw was his big bright smile! I was introduced to Dada in the lobby of JRB where he was told that my ancestors were Indians and Dada's response was, "So you are also an Indian". They also told Dada that I had pledged to be a vegetarian on Wednesdays. Dada asked me to be a vegetarian for life. I promised him I would be a vegetarian for the rest of his stay here at JRB. I have faithfully been a vegetarian for the last two weeks and I realize how much more energy I have and I am also sleeping a lot better at night.

On Sunday June 26, 2010 I was cleaning Dada's apartment and Dada was sitting in the library. I was quickly going in and out of his apartment and I realized that his bright smile was giving me a peace within, that I have never felt before. I gently went to him and took his hand in mine and said, "Dada, you have blessed me". His reply was "No, God has blessed you". I said to Dada, "You and God have blessed me!" and he thanked me with that big smile on his face.

At about 1PM today (June 30, 2010) I was reading one of Dada's books where he teaches "Anger ceaseth not by anger"; the person who forgives enters a new life of gentle peacefulness. To read this is just what I needed today. Dada – thank you for your wisdom and your blessings.

Ms. Floret
Rush University Medical Center

When I met Dada he had no less than four broken bones and had just endured a long plane ride. Despite all his suffering he was already demonstrating his strength and strong will to heal. We told him all the surgery he would need, and he never even flinched! I told him that the recovery would be long and difficult: he said that was fine, he was ready. Despite all he went through during his stay with us, he never complained, never showed frustration, and never stopped working hard. He was always gracious and kind to all our staff, and it was nearly impossible to leave his room without some gift. His determination and sense of humour were with him up to the last day we saw him before his departure. We wish him well; he was truly a pleasure to have as a patient.

Dr. Walter Virkus, MD
Associate Professor Orthopaedic Surgery
Orthopaedic Trauma and Oncology
Midwest Orthopaedics at Rush

It has been my privilege, a distinct honour and an enlightening experience to be in the service of Revered Dada for almost fifteen years.

Poojya Dada is always very calm, composed, peaceful and cheerful under the most painful and extenuating circumstances. No matter how serious the problem has been, his kind smile and charming personality remain unchanged and that can change the demeanour of any person who comes in contact with Dada.

Dada's positive thinking and cooperative spirit has been a very important ingredient in his recovery. His unconditional love, humility and kindness are sure to touch everyone's heart. It is easy to see why everyone who comes in contact with him has a pleasant, spiritual experience and develops love and devotion for respected Dada.

We pray to God for Dada's speedy recovery.

With Deepest Regards for Dada

Dr. Ramesh Chhablani, M.D, F.A.C.C
Senior Attending Cardiologist
Division of Cardiology
Rush University Medical Center

Dada's fall is but a rise!

Since May 7th when our Revered Dada sustained the fall in Panama, I have been agonizing over just one question— why do 'bad' things happen to great people? In the ensuing several weeks of pain, suffering and intense efforts at rehabilitation, what has most touched all of us is that Dada has remained cool, calm, comfortable, and composed. His mystic smile, his quick wit, and his genuine love for all around him permeate the atmosphere in the hospital at all times. More often, he is most concerned about how his devotees are faring in their daily struggles of life rather than his own pain and discomfort.

His physicians, nurses and therapists at the hospital have all been impressed with his positive energy during this period of crisis. He is always upbeat, always full of hope, and always filled with a tremendous sense of gratitude. He humbly and smilingly bows to the will of the Lord. His rise from this fall has been a great lesson for each one of us. We feel strengthened in our belief that Dada will attain full recovery in the next few months, so as to be able to continue his divine mission of showing us the way in this mysterious journey of life.

Dr. Gopal Lalmalani, MD, FACC, FCCP, MBA
Chairman, Bylaws Committee, Advocate Good Samaritan Hospital, Downer's Grove, Illinois.
Director, Division of Cardiology, Loretto Hospital, Chicago, Illinois.
President, Midwest Cardiac Center, S.C., Lombard, Illinois.

———————

We had the opportunity to meet Dada Jashan Vaswani when he arrived to Rush Hospital after his severe injuries in early May. We treated his elbow injury and performed a total elbow replacement so he could regain use of his elbow. Through out his stay with us, Dada was very strong and determined to recover quickly. He was an inspiration to all those that worked alongside him. Our thoughts and prayers are with him, and we hope for his earliest recovery.

Dr. Gopal Lalmalani, MD
Director, Hand and Elbow Section
Midwest Orthopaedics at Rush

———————

From my very first meeting with Dada Vaswani, I immediately knew I was in the presence of a divine individual. Dada was extremely humble and gracious to me. I was fortunate to be in his presence and he made me feel as if he was lucky to be in my presence. Dada always has a kind word, an infectious smile and an optimistic and encouraging demeanour. Even during the most intense discomfort and pain imaginable, he never lost his graciousness. Dada has an energy and zest for life that we can all emulate. I have been fortunate to have been in Dada's presence and anyone who has met Dada has experienced the same. Our lives are enriched by him and his life is a model for us to aspire to.

Dr. Kousik Krishnan, MD, FACC
Assistant Professor of Medicine
Director, Arrhythmia Device Clinic
Rush University Medical Center
Chicago, IL 60612

How did I feel working with Dada? Answering this question had me thinking. As a Physical Therapist, I admit that at first, I was not sure if I could help Dada walk again. But, Dada's smile took all the 'ifs' away and his determination, motivation and willingness to work hard made me push and challenge him. He never showed signs of frustration. He was always grateful to everyone and very appreciative. He was the perfect example of an ideal patient.

What draws me to Dada, over and above my role as a Physical Therapist, is hard to explain. Is it because of the awe and love that I see from the people surrounding him? Is it his wonderful smile? Is it because I am hoping to have a connection to heaven? It is all of this and something more, which is hard to explain. Dada just has a certain enigma. There is an irresistible pull towards Dada that is very hard to resist. What it is, is indescribable.

Dada, remember, all that I want from you, is for you to get better and better: that will be the best present you can give me.

Ms. Caroline Saavedra
Physical Therapist
Rush University Medical Center